TEACHING MUSIC WITH PURPOSE

Conducting, Rehearsing and Inspiring

PETER LOEL BOONSHAFT

Published by
MEREDITH MUSIC PUBLICATIONS
a division of G.W. Music, Inc.
4899 Lerch Creek Ct., Galesville, MD 20765
http://www.meredithmusic.com

MEREDITH MUSIC PUBLICATIONS and its stylized double M logo
are trademarks of
MEREDITH MUSIC PUBLICATIONS, a division of G.W. Music, Inc.

International Standard Book Number: 1-57463-076-8
Library of Congress Control Number: 200693032
Printed and bound in U.S.A

DEDICATION

For my wife, Martha, and my children, Meredith Ann, Peter Loel and Matthew Christopher. Thank you for the joy you bring me. Thank you for allowing me to share your love and laughter. You are all that is wonderful in my life. It is said that one should "Be of love, a little more careful than of everything." When I look at each of you, I know why. Thank you for making me who I am and who I hope to be. No words can express the depth of my love for each of you.

ACKNOWLEDGEMENTS

To Dr. Garwood Whaley, Bruce Bush, Reber Clark and Nancy Bittner, thank you for your counsel, wisdom, support, patience and talents, but most of all, for your enduring friendship.

To James Swearingen, thank you for your constant encouragement, for the gift of your talents and spirit, and for writing the foreword to this book. Thank you for your sincerity, kindness and passion for music and education. Thank you for being you, my dear friend.

To my family, friends and colleagues, thank you for your thoughtfulness and inspiration.

And, most importantly, thank you to all of my students, who have given me the privilege and honor of learning from them. I hope you know how much I appreciate and cherish each of you, always.

CONTENTS

FOREWORD

In the course of a lifetime, nearly all of us meet people that affect us in a highly positive manner. "Life-changing" is often the way we describe these special encounters. As a composer of educational band literature, I've traveled the world over, and many outstanding people have come in and out of my life. Peter Boonshaft, for whatever wonderful reason, has remained a constant. A person has never had a better friend or colleague. I strongly suspect that one of the primary reasons is his unique ability to lift my spirits and make me laugh when I'm feeling down. In so doing, Peter's kind words of support have often served as an inspiration to move immediately from one's own set of problems in order to focus on the far greater good of helping others.

Peter is a person of great wisdom, yet his message, while thought provoking, is never complicated or difficult to comprehend. Reflective of the master teacher that he is, this approach has served him extremely well when students and teachers of all ages, abilities and backgrounds have sought his expertise and guidance. In addition, he is always willing to give of his time, and his sincere ability to make others feel far more important in his presence is a quality that I find rare and truly exceptional in this age of *"it's all about me."*

For all of Peter's talents with the spoken and written word, I continue to be increasingly astounded by his extraordinary talent as a conductor. Peter's artistic gestures speak volumes with regard to making a musical performance come *"to life."* His deep passion for music and the immense size of his heart are at the very core of his success.

Teaching Music with Purpose is a tremendous gift from a man who has spent years working to hone his craft. In this book, Peter Boonshaft intimately shares a collection of personal experiences with tried-and-true teaching techniques that are sure to touch the human spirit in ways that go far beyond the basics of teacher training. Quite simply, he embraces the magic ingredient of caring in the noble *"art"* of teaching.

All of the qualities about Peter that I thoroughly appreciate come across very clearly in this magnificent book. Sit back, enjoy and learn from a person who, on a daily basis, actively demonstrates a profound conviction for the profession and art that he so dearly loves. Needless to say, you're in for a real treat and a tremendous learning experience. You should also be forewarned that you might find yourself laughing or crying at a moment's notice, yet, for all the right reasons. Above all else, be prepared to discover, like me, an association with a friend that is sure to last for many years to come!

James Swearingen
Chair, Department of Music Education
Capital University

PREFACE:
A LITTLE OLD MAN WHO KNEW

It was the beginning of September. I was eighteen years old, a freshman in college. There I sat, in an auditorium filled with music students, awaiting the start of our opening convocation. Not knowing what to expect, I wondered how it would begin. Would it start with the playing of a fanfare by the brass choir, a rousing anthem by the chorus, or a stirring overture by the symphony orchestra? Would the pipe organ resonate with celebratory strains? Would herald trumpets announce the start of this regal occasion? Would there be pomp and ceremony? Would the faculty process onto the stage wearing long black robes complete with academic hoods? I wondered.

Finally, the lights dimmed, and I realized I was about to find out. After a moment or two, onto the stage shuffled a little old man wearing a tattered old sweater. No robes, no trumpets, no pageantry, no celebration. Just a little old man who looked to be somewhere between 90 and 160 years of age. A little, unassuming old man who would become one of my greatest teachers. There stood the little old man who would change my life.

"When I was twenty-one," he began, "I knew *everything*. When I was thirty-one, I discovered I could learn a bit more about one or two things. When I was forty-one, I realized there were a *few* things I didn't know. At fifty-one, I recognized there were *many* things I didn't know. At sixty-one, I knew there was a lot I still needed to learn. At seventy-one, I conceded there was more I *didn't* know, than I *did* know. And now I stand here before you, at the age of eighty-one, confident that I don't know *anything*."

I sat there mesmerized as this gentle old man proceeded to talk about the educational journey before us. He spoke about the virtues of hard work, the need to persevere, the importance of patience, the incredible value of every second of time, the beauty of our art and the splendor of a life dedicated to music. He spoke passionately, reverently, powerfully. But this wasn't a speech. It wasn't just heartfelt wisdom. This was the evangelical plea of an old man who didn't want any of us—not one person in this auditorium full of young people—to waste a single moment of life. Life, that with each passing day, he found more precious.

Later, I discovered the little old man was the dean emeritus of the school of music, the musical elder-statesman of the university. The years of studying with him, watching him, hearing him perform, and playing under his baton taught me more than words can say. He taught me as much about what music *could be* as he did about what music *was*. He taught me to learn as much as possible, wherever I could, whenever I could, from whomever I could. He taught me to work hard, and to make as much music as I could, with all my heart and soul. But mostly, he taught me that someday, if I were lucky, very lucky, I could stand in front of a group of students at the ripe old age of eighty-one and declare the fact that I, too, knew nothing.

I also came to learn that every year would begin this way. Though he, and his age in the story, would grow older with each passing year, the spirit and conviction of his message seemed to grow stronger. Every year, an auditorium full of new young people would sit there, and whether they knew it or not, they would bear witness to the indomitable character, the resolute force that was this little old man. A little old man, with a tattered old sweater, who changed my life by teaching me what he *didn't know*, as much as he did with what he *did know*. A little old man who embodied the words of the great Michelangelo, who at the age of eighty-seven said, "Ancora imparo," simply, "Still I am learning."

It is with that spirit, and the belief that those who think they have all the answers don't really know the questions, this book was written. There are no answers here, no right or better way to do anything. What follows is simply food for thought, ideas to mull over. Some ideas you will recognize as *what you do* and *who you are* every day. Some you will recognize as "old friends" not thought about for a while you may decide to revisit. Some may be new and worth consideration, while others may cause us to disagree strongly.

And do you know what? All of those possibilities are wonderful. For what could be better than for each of us to confirm our thoughts, challenge our beliefs and strengthen our resolve? Sometimes, trying new ideas or thinking new thoughts can be more liberating than enlightening, more creatively thought-provoking than instructional. Especially if we always remember that the *right way* isn't always the opposite of the *wrong way*.

All any of us can do is spend our lives asking questions, searching for answers, trying new ideas, testing, seeking, looking, exploring, aspiring for better. Better for ourselves, our students, our communities, our art and our world. A world every teacher changes one student at a time. And in so doing, we honor those who have entrusted themselves to us, just like we entrusted ourselves to those who taught us.

I guess it all boils down to shoulders. Yes, you read correctly, *shoulders*. More precisely, being *appreciative* of shoulders. For teachers—we whose purpose it is to take the knowledge of the past, add to it, then pass it on to the next generation to do the same—no words could be more perfect than those of Sir Isaac Newton: "If I have seen farther, it is by standing upon the shoulders of giants." I am so appreciative of the giants in my life—my family, friends, colleagues, teachers and students—who have allowed me to see by my standing upon their wise and talented shoulders. They have taught me and will always continue to teach me.

In fact, this book is a collection of that which I have learned from my teachers and students. It also contains many quotes from people far more learned than I will ever be. Every effort has been made to correctly attribute those thoughts; however, where the author is believed to be unknown, no ascription has been made.

I also want to thank *you* for reading these pages, and sharing with me the journey that is teaching and learning. Words do not exist that express my appreciation for your kindness and support. My thanks for all you do as teachers, mentors and musical beacons is matched only by my awe at your commitment, dedication and talents. On behalf of every student whose life you touch, thank you. Thank you for what you do and who you are, but, even more, for that which you help your students to learn and who you help them to become. No purpose could be greater than that. No journey could be more joyous. And rich is the person who spends their life so nobly, with such purpose.

"Purpose." What an amazing word. A word I chose for the title of this book because of its various and wonderful meanings, every aspect of which we—as teachers—personify. For indeed, we teach with the purpose of perseverance, determination and drive; the purpose that is our intent, end and goal; and the purpose that is our reason, rationale and principle. But what *is* our purpose? What is the *purpose* of teaching music?

Each of us answers those questions in our own way every time we stand before a room full of students, every time we look into their eyes, every time we encourage them to touch the stars, every time we help them reveal their souls, every time we get them to cry or laugh, every time we make them realize the wonder and greatness that is them.

Amazing, isn't it? All that from a bunch of little black dots on a page of white, and a person who cares more than others can conceive. We call them teachers. Those people who selflessly dedicate their lives to a profoundly fantastic journey. May the journey of your teaching be as magnificent and full of wonder as those students with whom you share it.

"...a journey."

FROM MUDDY WATERS

I had a dream once that I was conducting a fifth grade band. It was our first rehearsal. As I started to conduct, they began to play David Holsinger's *To Tame the Perilous Skies*. And let me tell you, they didn't just "play" it, they performed it magnificently. It was truly amazing. It was also a dream. Now there was some truth to my dream. I had worked with a fifth grade band earlier that day. They truly needed to be "tamed," and there was much in that rehearsal which sounded quite "perilous." However, that is where the similarities stopped.

Don't we all wish we could stand in front of our ensembles and have any composition performed flawlessly at sight? Yes, maybe deep down we might, but every teacher knows our true calling is to take students from where they are and move them to where we know they can go. Wherever they may be when we get them, we must nurture and encourage each of them to "Bloom where you are planted." Is it easy? Of course not. But our challenge is to follow the admonition of Theodore Roosevelt: "Do what you can, with what you have, where you are."

We do that every day, knowing that what we do and how we do it will impact our students far more powerfully than any knowledge or skill. Our teaching is more far-reaching, influential and enduring than we can imagine. Every day is filled with frustrations, but every day is also filled with promise: not just for what we will teach our students, but also for how we will impact their lives. Each time we stand in front of them, we must remember Graham Greene's words: "There is always one moment in childhood when the door opens and lets the future in." That is the profound power of what we do. We can make *that moment* for each of our students. A moment they may not even realize for years, when, in the middle of a music class, lesson or rehearsal, *we* opened a door and helped them to let their future in.

Sometimes, as we all know, it is difficult to keep that in mind. Once I overheard one of my college students who had just finished his first day of apprentice teaching say to an underclassman, "Nothing really prepares you for the sound of a beginning band at their first rehearsal. Nothing!" I couldn't help but laugh at the truth of those words. It is amazing. You can observe for years, but nothing prepares you for your first time in front of that ensemble. Nothing! I usually refer to that sound as a musical amoeba: I don't really know what it is, it seems to spread like wildfire and I'm pretty sure it isn't very good for your health.

And though that same group may someday sound as pure as a crystal clear spring-fed stream, at that moment it sounds more like a muddy swamp. Well, when you hear those muddy waters, think of the wonderful Zen teaching which reminds us that the amazingly exquisite lotus flower grows only in swamps or marshes, rising out of those muddy waters to bloom with almost unimaginable beauty.

We must reach down to where our students are, no matter how "muddy" that is, and help them to bloom. Knowing, as John Andrew Holmes observed, "There is no exercise better for the heart than reaching down and lifting people up."

That's the funny thing about teachers. We have the ability to hear the most ghastly sounding ensemble and get excited at the thought of transforming them into something beautiful. Where the average human being would run away from those sounds, we savor the opportunity to help. It reminds me of a visit to a state music education convention. As I was walking down a hallway, I happened by a room with sounds coming from it that were absolutely horrific. It was the warm-up room for the All-State Orchestra violinists before their seating auditions. All of them! Now, individually, I am sure they each played magnificently. And, as part of the orchestra, I am sure they were astounding. However, the sound of one hundred violinists, each playing his or her favorite excerpt or exercise at the same time, wafting down the hallway, sounded like the soundtrack of a horror movie. It was awful!

So there I was walking down that hallway. No other person in sight but one. As this stranger and I passed the room, she reverently said, "Ah, isn't that a marvelous sound!" And you know what? She was right. To the average person, it was noise at best. To a music teacher it was promise, hope, joy, success and the future, all rolled into one. What gene were we born with which allows us to perceive *that* sound as beautiful? I don't know, but she was right: it *was* marvelous!

Why do some people see an empty jar as trash, while others see it as a pencil holder, vase or penny bank? Vision: the ability to see what is invisible. Better still, being able to see something *that is* as what it *can be*. Pablo Picasso stated, "Some painters transform the sun into a yellow spot, others transform a yellow spot into the sun." We take the "yellow spots" that are our students and help them to become their best "sun." Picasso would have made a great music teacher!

We all know it's easier said than done. We all know it is never-ending work. But we also know it is our mission, our calling and a joy we wouldn't trade for anything. Will you encounter those who say it's futile or impossible? Sure, and when you do, just think to yourself, "People who say it cannot be done should not interrupt those who are doing it." So take that empty jar, fill it with yellow paint and transform that spot into the sun. Let it shine down its light on those muddy waters, and help a beautiful lotus flower to emerge from that swamp for all to see.

"EDUCATION IS FUNDAMENTALLY AN IMAGINATIVE ACT OF HOPE"

O f all the negative feelings we humans are capable of, what do you think is the worst? Hate? Anxiety? Fear? I believe the worst is *frustration*. I think it is the root cause of so many destructive emotions, especially for teachers. Frustration causes anxiety, burnout, apathy, anger and so many other roadblocks. At the very least it sidetracks each of us from being the teacher we want to be.

But let's face it, what we do is often frustrating. I certainly don't need to list all the sources of frustration we teachers face day in and day out. However, I think the one that is *most* worrisome to me is the frustration of where an ensemble is now *versus* where we want it to be. And the weaker we perceive the group to be, the worse that frustration seems. Knowing what it will take to move an ensemble best described as "The Honkers and Dingers" to where it needs to be can be discouraging to say the least.

Staying positive and hopeful in the face of educational hurdles is difficult, but doing so when faced with extraordinary challenges can sometimes put us over the edge. What follows are a few thoughts I have used as guides through those sometimes murky and confusing times.

Be Hopeful

No matter the cause of our frustration, we must remember those words of William Purkey and John Novak which title this chapter: "Education is fundamentally an imaginative act of hope." That really sums up everything I believe. It is the alpha and the omega of education. We're just a bunch of optimists, or we wouldn't be in this profession. Put simply, we just can't be frustrated with how badly they play or how little they know.

See Greatness

We can't lose sight of the fact that our job is to see the greatness in each of our students; not just in their ability, but in them as people. Sure, it's easy to see faults and shortcomings, but as their teachers, we must look deeper into their eyes and see the greatness that lies inside. Sometimes I think students don't show their greatness because no one has ever believed it was there.

Presume Excellence

Self-fulfilling prophecies work for each of us as people, but I think they work just as powerfully for us as teachers. If we presume a student or group of students will struggle to achieve, they *will* struggle to achieve. If we think an ensemble will end up being one of our weakest, it will. However, if we assume our students will be high achievers and expect they will excel, more than likely, they will. I know this sounds like so much psychobabble, but I believe it more than I can express. They *will* become what we think they will become. They will become the vision, however good or bad, of what we see in them.

Backwards Completion Principle

Sometimes the best way to get students to where we want them to be is to *envision them there*. Picture the goal point. Then plot backwards from there, step by step, to where they are now. Working from "finish" to "start" can sometimes be exhilarating and empowering.

Believe in Them

They must be convinced that *you are convinced* they will achieve the goal. Sometimes it is less about their believing they can, and more about their believing *we believe* they can! Students can't, unless we help them believe they can.

Stepping Stones

Every new challenge our students face along their paths can be seen as a stepping stone *or* as a stumbling block; the former serving to lift them up, the latter to knock them down. We have to convince them those "bars" we keep raising are steps to their success rather than obstacles in their path.

Facilitated Expectations

When we come to a rehearsal with an expectation, a goal, do we also come with a procedure to get there? In other words, do we facilitate accomplishing that goal with a lesson plan to make it happen? If students are given a planned, prioritized procedure to get there, they *can* do it. Expectations alone are lofty ambitions; facilitated expectations are a staircase to success.

Take a Giant Step Backwards

When students sense they are playing poorly, they can become like mules: very hard to move forward, very willing to stay put. If we start them with music so "easy" they sound good, or can sound good in short order, they start to become like the little engine that could: thinking they can. It's so easy for our students to "throw in the towel" when *they think* they are already defeated. However, it is also easy for them to become motivated by early success.

Think of it like dieting. Sadly, I have had more than my fair share of dieting, so I can speak as an expert. Ask anyone who has dieted; it's easy to stay motivated in the first few days because the pounds fall off with relative ease. Success breeds success, so we stay on track with enthusiasm. The problem comes after a few days, when the plateaus start and frustration sets in. Perceived frustration breeds a feeling the goal cannot be achieved, which makes it very, very easy to give up. Then it's donut shop here I come!

Even if that means your high school band starts the year with "Hot Cross Buns" in whole notes, so be it, if it allows them to play musically and thereby sense the beauty of music and the joy of excellence. Sometimes a step backwards can make possible many steps forward.

Vitamins: The Right Prescription

I take vitamins every day. I have for years. I am earnest about it. But why? Why do I take them? I don't know if they are doing anything for me. I have never seen any immediate results or specific effects from them, the way I have from aspirin or antibiotics. So why take them? Well, I hope that by taking them every day, they will build up in my body and keep me healthy. At some point they may keep me from getting some awful disease. But I really don't know. Again, it all comes down to hope. I am willing to stick with it, confident in the knowledge they are the right prescription—a prescription that will pay off in the future.

Basic fundamentals are the "vitamins" of music education. All that work on posture, sound production, intonation, breathing, steadiness of pulse, phrasing, hand position, embouchure, bow arm, balance, blend, internal subdivision, diction and the like, are the vitamins C, B1 and D of music teaching. Can we know when they will yield results? No. Will their benefits be immediately seen? Maybe not. But good fundamentals are the *sine qua non* of education.

Which Frog?

Sometimes the weakest starters end up being the best finishers. And the truth is we don't really know which "frog," with the "kiss" of great teaching, will become a "prince." Even those who start as "frog" players or ensembles can become "prince" successes, if we measure success by how much they have progressed and their level of enjoyment. Funny thing about frogs: they might just end up sitting on a throne.

The Vinegar Tasters

The best way to summarize my feelings is to draw from a passage entitled "The Vinegar Tasters," as described by Benjamin Hoff in

The Tao of Pooh. Though its original purpose was to help shed light on three eastern philosophies, it clearly illuminates the ways we can view those moments we all have of "tasting vinegar." It's not just about optimism, but perspective, attitude and how we look at everything:

> We see three men standing around a vat of vinegar. Each has dipped his finger into the vinegar and has tasted it. The expression on each man's face shows his individual reaction. Since the painting is allegorical, we are to understand that these are no ordinary vinegar tasters, but are instead representatives of the "three teachings" of China, and that the vinegar they are sampling represents the Essence of Life. The three masters are K'ung Fu-tse (Confucius), Buddha, and Lao-tse, author of the oldest book of Taoism. The first has a sour look on his face, the second wears a bitter expression, but the third man is smiling.

Every minute we teach, we have the opportunity to interpret what we have before us as sour, bitter or *sweet*. It is entirely up to us. Those three men sampled from the same vat, they drank the same liquid; they just tasted it very differently. If we always view teaching as that imaginative act of hope, we will have no choice but to smile when we encounter that which is sour, bitter or sweet. ■

DWELLING ON DREAMS

It does not do to dwell on dreams and forget to live..." said Albus Dumbledore in J. K. Rowling's *Harry Potter*. A wise man, that Dumbledore. Truer words could not be spoken for just about everything in life, but for us as teachers, that quite possibly represents the hardest balancing act of our profession. If you think about it, it is almost schizophrenic. On one hand, we want our students to enjoy their accomplishments and take pleasure in the success of the moment. We know the value of having them review what they have learned and enjoy the fruits of their labor.

On the other hand, we have a constant desire to push them to higher and higher levels of accomplishment. Then we become so worried about getting them to the goal, we forget—and we allow them to forget—to enjoy the process. The enjoyment of the steps along the way, the beauty along the path they take to their accomplishments, is lost to the goal of getting there. We spend so much effort "dreaming" of future accomplishments for our students that we forget to "live" and enjoy each moment.

But on the third hand, isn't a central part of our mission to help our students achieve higher and higher levels of accomplishment? If so, every moment counts. We can't spend time smelling flowers along the way; we have to get to the top of the mountain.

Still, on the fourth hand, we know that our students' time with us must be enjoyable. There certainly has to be hard work at times, but we can never allow it to become debilitating. Too much of that and we know we will lose them—in every way.

This reminds me of a dining experience I had years ago at a very fancy restaurant. About six of us were invited to go to dinner with a local celebrity who owned the establishment. This gentleman was obviously respected by his employees who did everything, and I mean everything, to make us feel pampered. As we sat down, the staff started bringing food to us as if for a State Dinner: course after course after course. It became obvious this was to be a wonderful experience. It also became obvious that each of us had our own waiter or waitress. Really! It was amazing. I felt like a king.

So what does that story have to do with the teacher's balancing act referenced above? Well, the servers drove us crazy. In an effort to be ever vigilant, on top of things, and to make us feel cared for, they were taking away our plates as the forks brought the last bites to our mouths. Actually, very often they took the plate if they *sensed* you had stopped eating for a second, even if the plate was still full. Of course no one said anything, not wanting to offend our host, but it drove us all nuts. The sense of frustration was overwhelming. A delightful plate of some beautiful creation was placed in front of us. We were told to savor it. Then, before we could swallow, it was taken away. I was never given the chance to enjoy the moment, because the staff wanted us to complete as many courses as was possible. In their minds, we *had* to finish the meal...every single course. A wonderful goal, but it left each of us frustrated.

I guess the bottom line is that we can never lose our desire to push our students further, but it must be managed so perspective is also never lost. That is what it's all about. We must keep sight of the goal and constantly encourage growth, but never allow it to loom so greatly as to be daunting. That goal can never overshadow the enjoyment of learning or the joy of what has been learned. Perspective, though, is a funny thing: it seems so obvious and logical, until tested.

We know our students' well-being is what is truly important. Whether they get to dessert or only get as far as the third appetizer, they must learn to taste every morsel along the way and enjoy it. They need to be proud of their effort and ability, all the while being reminded of the amazing things still ahead of them.

I think it comes down to helping students know that sometimes, as Dale Carnegie stated, "Success is getting what you want. Happiness is wanting what you get." We must help students balance *both* of those. It is a balancing act which is the responsibility of every teacher. When I get impatient, as often happens, I remember the following words of wisdom:

A Child
is a butterfly in the wind…
Some can fly higher than others
But each one flies the best that it can!
Why compare one against the other?
Each one is different…
Each one is special…
Each one is beautiful….

They help keep me on the path I want for my students. They help keep me on the path I want for *myself*. In their awesome power is the truth of our mission:

A hundred years from now...
it will not matter what my bank account was, the sort of house I
lived in, or the kind of car I drove...
...but the world may be different because I was important in the
life of a child.

THE "BIG ROCKS" CONCEPT

A science teacher presented an empty bucket to his students, then filled it with big rocks. Showing it to the class, he asked them if the bucket was full. They answered, "Yes!" He then added medium-sized rocks to the bucket, whereupon those rocks dropped down and filled in the places around the big rocks. He again asked the class if the bucket was full. Now catching on, the class somewhat reticently responded, "Yes?" Then the teacher added small rocks that took their place in the spaces around the medium rocks. Again, the teacher asked the class if the bucket was full, to which they less than confidently said, "Yes." The teacher then added sand to the bucket, filling the bucket to the very brim, allowing the tiny grains to fill every crevice of space around even those small rocks. The teacher asked his class if the bucket was now full. They joyfully responded, "Yes!" At that moment the teacher held up a pitcher of water and began pouring it into the bucket. The water trickled down and touched every rock and every grain of sand, now filling the bucket. Then, and only then, was the bucket truly full.

How amazing. How profound. How true. A dear friend of mine shared that story with me sometime ago. It is based on the notion put forth by Stephen Covey in his book *First Things First*. After hearing it, I was awestruck at the power of its message, and how it served as a perfect metaphor for learning, teaching, growing and living. In its simplicity can be found a lesson for us to share with our students, a lesson far more valuable than meets the eye.

The "Big Rocks" of Teaching Music

This "bucket" starts with the "big rocks" of posture, position (finger, hand, arm, body, embouchure, etc.) and breathing, those bedrock concepts that serve as a foundation for success. To it we add the "medium rocks" of that quintessentially important concept: tone production. Then we add the "small rocks" of technique, and the "sand" of musical performance concepts. Finally, the "water" of all that is truly important: infusing every sound with feeling and expression, the true purpose all along.

The "Big Rocks" of Rehearsing

The "big rocks" that fill this "bucket" are "what's on the page," the black and white of music: the notes and symbols. To that we add the "medium rocks" of ensemble performance concepts like balance, blend, intonation, diction, bowing, articulation and phrasing. Then we add the "small rocks" of musical detail and a better sense of ensemble, and the "sand" of nuance, subtlety and contrast. To what end? So we can breathe life into the composition by adding the "water" of emotion, meaning, power and passion. To connect every surface of each rock of "technique" for its real purpose: to make meaningful, expressive, artistic communication.

The "Big Rocks" of What We Really Teach

We fill this "bucket" with the "big rocks" of teaching music to students. Then we add the "medium rocks" of all the other subjects and skills we teach or reinforce. To that we add the "small rocks" of the life skills we teach: work ethic, *esprit de corps*, self-discipline, the meaning of community, selflessness, pride, overcoming obstacles, reaching for goals, and striving for the very best. Next, the "sand" of helping them develop the *people* they will become, and see the wonder and miracle they are. We then pour from the pitcher of our encouragement, love, compassion and dedication the "water" of dreams, aspirations and the appreciation of life and living. That "water" connects every surface of every "rock" of fact, every "grain" of learning, to help mold caring, feeling, thriving, joyful people.

The "Big Rocks" Concept of "Buckets"

But, quite possibly, that story is best a metaphor for our abilities, our capacity for growth and achievement. Even when we think we have "filled" our "bucket," rarely have we. And I figure even if we do *really* fill that "bucket" we can always just get a bigger one and start from there. So it goes: the never-ending filling of a pail, the never-ending quest for becoming still better than we already are. Perhaps that is quite simply the way of life: first to place the "big rocks" in our "bucket" and then work to fill it better. █

IT'S ALL IN HOW YOU
SEE IT

The bell just rang. It's now three o'clock in the afternoon. The school day has ended. As usual, before leaving for home, you have many things to do and a million thoughts running through your head: "I need to find a better warm-up exercise to help reinforce rhythmic subdivision for my seventh-grade band. What can I do to 'reach' Steve and Bill and Sue? What can I say to convince the trumpets that I believe in their ability to get that lick? I need to find a 'tone piece' for my eighth-grade band. If Fred cracks the top of his solo again I'll scream. When will the trumpets ever learn that accidentals carry through the bar? Boy did Joe mess up that run-through of *Chester* by missing every cymbal crash. If I have to tell the trombones to play louder one more time. I am so tired of trying to convince the eighth-grade band the joys of playing soft and elegant as opposed to high, fast and loud. If only my school principal could understand why music is so important. One more sixth-grade-humor joke in band and I'll die." Thoughts like those, and more than this book could contain.

Only this day is different. It is the day you retire from teaching. This day you will pack up your things, turn off the light and lock your classroom for the last time. The door will close. You will turn that key as you always have. But this time, knowing you will never return, the sound of the lock rings out like a *sforzando* strike on a bass drum. At that moment, everything changes. Now, as you walk out of the building, those earlier thoughts change. They are suddenly transformed into: "I'll miss the challenge of finding a better warm-up exercise to help reinforce rhythmic subdivision for my seventh-grade band. When Steve, Bill and Sue finally 'get it' they will be remarkable. I'll miss giving those pep-talks to the trumpets, trying to convince them anything is possible. I just thought of the perfect 'tone piece' for the eighth-grade band, but I'll never get to hear them play it. I'll miss the chance to smile from ear to ear when Fred plays that solo without a crack. One more day and I could have gotten the trumpets to remember the rule about accidentals. With another run-through of *Chester*, I could have conducted it in a way that would have helped show those cymbal crashes better. I'll miss those trombones and the looks on their faces when I told them to play louder and they responded by holding their trombones like bazookas with my head as the target. I'll miss the utter joy in the eyes of the eighth-grade band members when they finally play that soft, slow and elegant piece so well they feel something inside themselves they didn't even know existed. I wish I had put my principal on the podium so he would have heard what I heard and saw what I saw. I'll miss the silly sixth-grade jokes and the chance to see those who told them turn into adults."

What changed? They are the same trumpets and trombones, the same cymbal player and principal, the same bands with the same problems. What changed is our perspective. Do we now view things the same way we did on our first day of teaching? Do you remember the very first trumpet player you taught, the first day of your teaching career? Do you remember how excited you were and how much you reveled in the process of teaching? Do you remember the thrill it gave you? Do you remember the look on that student's face? Do you remember the utter joy you felt when you realized that at last you were indeed a teacher? Nothing has changed. Has it? Trumpet players still need to be taught to play with better tone. They still look toward the teacher for that training. The band room still smells like a locker room. You still have that tie you had on your first day of teaching. So what changed?

When we hear a trumpet player with "awful" tone, we can view the glass as half empty and think to ourselves: "I have to fix that again?" Or we can view the same glass as half full and think: "I get the chance to help him improve by teaching him techniques that will help him grow." Simply, we must *embrace* the *opportunities* to *teach*. We must relish the joys of the teaching, not just the moments when something has been learned. As Hugh Prather so aptly stated, "Happiness is a present attitude and not a future condition."

Some of the most profound words I know are those of Betty Smith, who said, "Look at everything as if you were seeing it either for the first time or the last time. Then your time on earth will be filled with glory." If we follow that sage advice, we will know our time on earth as teachers will be glorious, enjoyable and empowering. The next time you look at those students of yours, and see the "same old problems" while sighing at the very thought of fixing them, realize you have a choice. View those problems with disdain and fatigue, or with excitement and enthusiasm. Just remember the words of Ashleigh Brilliant: "Strangely enough, this is the past that somebody in the future is longing to go back to."

I always try to keep Herb Gardner's remarkable admonition in mind: "You have got to own your days and name them, each one of them, every one of them, or else the years go right by and none of them belong to you." How do we "own" our days as teachers? By reveling in the opportunities to teach, savoring the chance to impact young lives and remembering the successes. Then, after the years have gone by, all of those days *will* belong to us, as will the memories of those students and what we helped them to become as musicians and as people.

What you do, how you do it, and how you feel about it changes when you simply "Look at everything as if you were seeing it either for the first time or the last time." I dare say the day we lock our classroom for the last time we will remember the day we unlocked it for the first time. I hope we make all the days in between filled with the same sense of awe.

It is, quite simply, all in how we choose to see it. Maybe it comes down to following the wisdom of that renowned philosopher Ziggy, when he profoundly counseled, "You can complain because roses have thorns, or you can rejoice because thorns have roses."

"MOTIDISPIRATION": MOTIVATION, DISCIPLINE AND INSPIRATION

Motivation, Discipline and Inspiration. I wonder if any three words have been used more in the history of education. Some people think of them as separate concepts, while others believe they are related. I, however, don't just think they are related, I think they are one and the same; three sides, if you will, of the same coin. So I decided we needed a new word to describe that view, hence *motidispiration*: a blend of motivation, discipline and inspiration. Let me explain.

A great concern of so many teachers is controlling an ensemble, thereby creating a disciplined environment. And let's face it, that environment of ours is unique in education. As my wife often says, "Where else do you have eighty students in one room, each armed with a noisemaker?" Think about it; we're crazy. Not only do we revel in that situation, we stay up nights trying to figure out ways to get more students with more noisemakers. That scenario alone can create discipline challenges. For other teachers, however, controlling an ensemble is not a worry. They seem to do it naturally.

It doesn't matter which of those two we are, because motidispiration is the key, not only to creating a disciplined environment, but to getting to the next level. No matter how good or bad our ensembles are, it is the path to ever-greater heights. Whether it's taking a group from weak to better, or excellent to brilliant, motidispiration is the key that unlocks the door every ensemble must walk through. Simply, I define motidispiration as *progress or growth through controlled training, then teaching, to inspire students to be more motivated.* I like to think of it as the "Motidispiration Cycle," a six-part design for infusing inspiration and causing motivation, thus lessening the need for discipline.

Discipline: a word that nowadays seems synonymous with bad. A word that at once can make students grimace while putting a knot in the stomach of their teacher. A word that can just ruin a teacher's rehearsal, let alone day. But it shouldn't. It *can* be a good word and an even better concept. The trick is to differentiate between two types of discipline.

Reactive discipline is the one with the terrible reputation, and deservedly so. It is bad, always bad. It is putting out the fires of poor behavior after they have started to burn. It is reacting to bad behavior, placing the teacher in the position of trying to "catch up" to those behaviors, leaving little time or energy for moving the group *along* the path of learning, because we spend so much of it just keeping them *on* that path.

Proactive discipline, however, is good. It is positive and necessary. It is how we control and focus an ensemble so our students want to move, let alone have no choice but to move, along that path. Proactive discipline is how we determine outcomes, set the stride, control the classroom. Surely we will encounter, and must be capable of handling, both types of discipline. In fact, the skills and techniques used to manage and deal with both types of discipline are identical; it is only the context that differentiates them.

The Motidispiration Cycle

Control Them. This is where we create that controlled environment, the precursor to success which will move our students along the path to motivation. We must harness them, quiet and settle them, get them to be still, stop their fidgeting, focus their attention on us. This is where we get them to muster their intensity and concentration in anticipation of hard work.

Many years ago I watched an interview with the principal of an elementary school who in precious few years had taken the school's test scores and truancy rates from one of the worst to one of the best in that city. When asked her secret, this very intense woman looked at her interviewer and in an almost scoldingly solemn way declared, "Learning cannot exist in chaos." How true. Learning, let alone growth, security, confidence and expression cannot flourish in educational chaos.

Nowhere is this described better than in *The Seven Mysteries of Life* by Guy Murchie. He illustrates with profound wisdom and insight what we, as teachers, know to be so very true when he wrote, "If a violin string is lying on a table loose and detached from any violin, some might suppose it 'free' because it is unconstrained. But what, one should ask oneself, is it 'free' to do or be? Certainly it cannot vibrate with beautiful music in such a condition of limpness. Yet if you just fasten one end of it to the tailpiece of the violin and the other to a peg in the scroll, then tighten it to its allotted pitch, you have rendered it free to play. And you might say that spiritually the string has been liberated by being tied tightly at both ends. For this is one of the great paradoxes of the world to be seen and tested on every side: the principle of emancipation by discipline."

Every time I read that passage I am reminded of its truth. We render our students free to make beautiful music, to express themselves and to speak from the heart through the control necessary for an ensemble to function. We make it possible for them to musically and emotionally communicate with each other and with us. But equally important is how that control *frees us.* For who truly can teach in an environment of chaos? Controlling them allows us to be the teacher we want to be, to teach what we need to teach, to explain, to emote, to enjoy, to savor, to grow. Released by that very control from the bondage of worry, anger and disappointment, we can enjoy our art and our students. To foster that environment, we can use the discipline techniques which follow to allow us to...

Train Them. This is where we train our students how to act, what to do and when, what is acceptable behavior and what is not. Notice I did not use the word *teach.* Much like training a pet, we need to instill in them actions and behaviors we want, and dissuade those we do not want. We can't assume our students know not to talk or chew gum in rehearsals, or that they need to have a pencil, mark their parts, watch the conductor, become silent when someone stands on the podium, or stop singing or playing when we stop conducting. All of those actions, and many more, need to be trained. When "Fido" was a puppy, we didn't assume he knew not to chew every slipper in our home. No, we trained him not to. We kindly, lovingly, dispassionately, methodically trained him. We need do the same for our students (well, not the slippers, but most everything else). That will allow us to...

Teach Them. Now controlled and trained, we can teach students what to do to improve, offering specific techniques, concepts and information for their collective and individual growth and progress. We are free to truly teach, unhampered by disruptive behaviors that can otherwise bog us down. That will allow us to...

Inspire Them. We must be intense, enthusiastic and show we are as dedicated to them as we are to the music. We must teach them how to get to the goal; but of greater value, we must explain the goal *and* its virtues. We have to convince them to try, ever improve, sense progress, never settle, feel emotions and find beauty all around them. How? Well, I think we do it by making something beautiful, what I have always referred to as a "pearl": getting them to perform something, no matter how tiny, that is magnificent. It can be as small as one attack, one release, one phrase, one chord. It doesn't matter what or how little, just that it is beautiful, giving us the opportunity to praise them, show our emotions and share moments of sheer joy. That will allow *them* to...

Motivate Themselves. Interesting isn't it? Did you notice this is the first time I said *them* rather than *us*? That's right, because we can't motivate anyone. The word "motivate" comes from the Latin "motum," which means "to move." If you think of it in terms of my wanting to move you from one place to another, I can only do that if I shove you or pick you up and carry you. And we all know how educationally unsound and ineffective, let alone damaging, that can be. We cannot motivate someone else; what we can do is inspire them to be motivated, *to move* themselves. In that way, we are living the words of William Butler Yeats who so perfectly reminds us, "Education is not the filling of a pail, but the lighting of a fire."

Certainly we hope that fire will come from within the student, and eventually it will, but sometimes a few sparks of enticement can help light the fire we seek. Extrinsic motivation, rewards our students earn for good behavior or positive growth, often serves to encourage and stimulate that conduct. It can be non-related extrinsic motivation, such as candy for learning an exercise, pizza for a successful rehearsal, extra credit for having a pencil, or a gold star for a lesson done well. It can also be related extrinsic motivation, such as getting to rehearse outside on the first spring day, having your photograph posted for being selected section of the week, getting to go to a concert, having a guest conductor or soloist come in, or getting to play that piece *they* love. The problem with extrinsic motivation, as we all know, is too much of it for too long a time can lead to the "candy" being the only reason for the action.

So, we need to wean them from, or at least reduce, extrinsic motivation, moving them over time toward intrinsic motivation: the self-driven desire to experience, excel and aspire because of how it makes *them* feel, the joy they receive, and their personal revelations of wisdom and beauty in music. Simply put, because *they want to.*

We need to get our students addicted to success. Even if at first it is progress made through the lure of extrinsic motivation, by experiencing success—technically or emotionally—those accomplishments generate the desire to do more. Yes, that may begin from a desire for more reward, but eventually the feelings of growth, progress, accomplishment and the expressive quality of music will be the catalyst for even more of the same. And when that happens, we will remove or at least lessen the number of ...

Discipline Problems. I think worrying about discipline problems is incorrect. It is like locking the gate after the horses have run away, like prescribing antibiotics after the patient has died. It is an autopsy. It may be the first line of defense, but it is the *last line* of offense. What made the student misbehave has not been attended to. Those problems are the result of a lack of motivation. We need to be *proactive* to remove the causes of poor behavior, but, more importantly, to *cause* good behavior. Our energies, therefore, should be used to inspire motivation. For if I am motivated to move myself, why would I be a discipline problem? Success or progress comes through inspiration and motivation, thus removing much of the potential for poor behavior and consequently the need for discipline.

Why Do Kids Misbehave?

Why *do* kids act badly? What would take an otherwise normal young person and make him or her be disruptive or troublesome? As oversimplified as it may sound, I think it all comes down to one reason: to get attention. We all want attention, and if we can't or don't get it when we behave, we're going to get it when we misbehave. That attention may come from the teacher in the form of a reprimand or from our classmates in the form of laughter. Either way, poor behavior gets rewarded. Why? Because of a simple fact of life: we'd all rather be *praised* than *punished*, but we'd all rather be *punished* than *ignored*. It could be that we are bored, frustrated or starving for recognition; we are going to act out to get that attention. One way or the other, we *will* get noticed.

Causes of Poor Behavior

So often, *we* cause the very behaviors we detest. Well, maybe we don't cause them, but we surely *facilitate* them. Combine our students' need for attention with certain things we do—or don't do—in rehearsal and sometimes the results can be dreadful. If we recognize the specific catalysts or causes of bad behavior which

follow, simply removing them, changing them or doing the opposite action may go a long way toward remedying the situation.

Poorly Paced Rehearsals. I love a very fast paced rehearsal.
I figure it helps keep people awake, though some of the best conductors I know have a slow pace. When the pace gets too slow,
however, the result can be disastrous, as can slow, boring speech
patterns and a conductor who has long delays after stopping an
ensemble, not ready to offer information or correct problems.

"Down time" is so often when kids get into trouble, misbehaving if they don't have something better to do. Down time
that occurs while we move between pieces and activities can be
eliminated by training students that this is the time to focus their
attention on the next piece; that they are to *silently* study the work,
just as we train them to do when sight-reading. To me, it is one
and the same. They should be reminding themselves of previous
errors, stumbling points and the like. Their focus *then* should be as
intense, if not more intense, than when actually playing the piece.

Long lectures also create down time. My advice: if we can't say
it in five words or less, we shouldn't say it. Without question, some
concepts and stories need time, but usually we go on for minutes
with what could be said in three words. And "minutes" are plenty
of time to get a spit ball loaded, aimed and fired!

Another cause of down time is spending too much time with one
person or section while others grow restless. We can guard against
this, but sometimes it may be necessary. In those cases, *time on task* is
the key. While working with the clarinet section on a long passage,
ask trumpet players to circle—and add up—all of a certain accidental
they were having trouble with. Then, after hearing the clarinets, ask
the trumpet players for the total number of circled notes, making them
accountable for that activity. Or, have other sections practice "fingering" silently, telling them you will hear the passage in a moment.

Poorly Planned Rehearsals. We need to keep students on task, to keep them busy (especially percussionists, who get their own chapter!), not with the quantity of what we have them do, but by the quality of what we have them do. For that to happen, we must have a clear agenda, a detailed course of action, and a well-thought-out lesson plan, all rooted in our preparation: knowing the material cold. As "location, location, location" is for great real estate, "preparation, preparation, preparation" is for a great rehearsal.

Problems also occur when we don't take into consideration attention span. Imogene Hilyard said, "A child's chronological age in years is equal to his or her attention span in minutes." Having worked with college students for all these years, I question whether she meant seconds, but in either case, it is so true. Think about it: a ninth-grader has about fourteen minutes. Use it wisely. That is not to say after the first fourteen minutes of rehearsal they will shut down, but rather they have fourteen minutes of intense concentration they can give you during the rehearsal. The trick is for us to spread those minutes throughout the rehearsal, interspersing periods of review or lighter work so as to have the entire rehearsal be fruitful and productive.

Too Much Routine. As I discussed in another chapter, though we need some routine for structure, too much can be deadly. When on autopilot, doing the same old routine they have down pat, our students can easily mess around.

Unfocused Start of Rehearsal. The cause of many rehearsals being unfocused is the way they start. A rehearsal that begins quickly, calmly and in a focused and controlled manner usually stays that way. Conversely, rehearsals that start in a sloppy and rambunctious manner never seem to gain focus. Most of the problem comes from the making of announcements, signing of forms, collecting of papers and the endless conversations students "have to have" at that moment about anything and everything. All the while, other students slip into a fidgety, distracted state.

I advocate *training* students so none of those things occur at the beginning of rehearsal. Students are to come in, get themselves ready, focus on the work at hand, but they are *not* to come near me. With no gaggle of students at the podium pecking at me, I am free to think, greet my students and demonstrate through my own focus what is expected. They can speak to me from their seats with pleasantries and questions about a piece, but nothing else. The only exceptions are for illness or if their instruments don't work. Other than that, everything else must wait for the end of rehearsal.

You may be thinking, "*Five minutes* of announcements, fund-raisers and forms is *five minutes*. What does it matter whether it's the first or last five minutes of the rehearsal?" It matters a lot. Psychologically and sociologically it makes all the difference in the world, not just for those five minutes, but how those five minutes impact the prevailing attitude of the entire rehearsal. It is as healthy and liberating for the students as it is for their teacher.

A Silent Start. I believe the first moments of any rehearsal set the behavior for that rehearsal. If we begin with a subtle, or not-so-subtle, din of student chatter we have to "talk over," that becomes the norm. That will typically be the quietest the ensemble will get. However, if the teacher accepts nothing short of silence at the start of rehearsal, he or she can use a comfortable voice and students come to realize only silence is acceptable. That becomes the norm students learn they must return to, every time the teacher stops. That "new normal" becomes standard rehearsal deportment. Starting rehearsal with anything less trains our students that chatter and noise—which the teacher must talk over—is perfectly all right.

Failure to Specify Rules. Students must know our expectations from the very first day they are with us. We can't wait until students break the rules to explain the rules to them. If we fail to clearly specify the rules and procedures for our rehearsals, how can our students be expected to follow them? We can't assume students know to get quiet the moment someone steps onto the podium; we must tell them and train them to do so. We can't explain the rules as they are being broken. We can't assume anything, we must *train* it.

Lack of Readiness. Little we do can be as frustrating and debilitating for our students, thus creating an invitation for poor behavior, as asking them to do something for which they lack the mental, physical or emotional readiness to succeed. It always ends badly when our students don't have the mental readiness to understand the work at hand, the physical readiness for technical demands far ahead of their means or the emotional readiness for discussions of content beyond their grasp. Certainly we need to mentally, physically and emotionally challenge and stretch our students. But when that mark is well overshot, many of our students will, at best, tune out or be stymied, while others will have the perfect reason to misbehave.

Tools for Success. Little could be more important for student achievement and our control of the classroom than sequencing *what* is to be learned, laying the ground work for progress and growth. If we have not previously taught our students the concepts, techniques and material now needed to succeed, they will not have the tools for that success. As well, not having music or playing on a broken instrument prevents participation, let alone success. Students will, in each of these cases, be doomed to fail and be frustrated, often acting out negatively on those feelings.

Eyes on the Score. When our eyes are on the score, rather than on our students, not only do we impede the success of our conducting, we make it nearly impossible to gauge or assess student behavior, giving them motive, opportunity and license to misbehave.

Unable to Communicate. If a student can't see the teacher due to an ensemble set-up which hinders direct sight lines, or can't hear the teacher who uses too soft a voice, he or she will become frustrated or give up altogether. We get the same result when students "can't understand" what we want because our directions or instructions are unclear. If they don't understand us, let alone can't see or hear us, we won't be able to communicate with them, engage them in rehearsals or keep them on task.

Getting Too Chummy. We as teachers all want our students to like us. But if we let them think of us as friends, or hesitate to discipline them because we want to be nice in order that they like us, we invite disaster. Yes, we want them to like us, but far more important is for them to *respect* us. As Ron Clark so perfectly asserted, "You can't discipline kids and not love them, and you can't love them and not discipline them. The two must go hand in hand."

A Time Bomb Ready to Explode. Ignoring a problem rarely makes it go away. But because disciplining is as debilitating, energy-zapping and unpleasant for us as it is for our students, we often ignore poor behavior. Then, after not reacting to that behavior, when we can't take it anymore, we explode like unstable dynamite, often *overreacting* to the behavior. Not only is that building up of anger as unhealthy as it is uncomfortable *for us*, the subsequent blowing up usually ends with our saying much we later regret.

But the worst part of this pattern of behavior is it trains students that they can get away with the poor behavior several times before they will be challenged. If you're starving and know you will get smacked on the hand only after the third or fourth time you get caught with your hand in the cookie jar, you're going to grab for the cookies. It's just in this case our students may be starving for *attention* rather than *food*.

Established Consequences. You know what I mean: those prescribed consequences or punishment for misbehaving, such as, "Students who forget their music will write a one page essay on why every fourth-grade student should play flute or saxophone rather than tuba or bassoon." I don't like students being armed with that much information—information they then can use to make a reasonably informed decision as to whether doing a bad behavior is worth it or not.

I just don't want my students equipped with those facts. A little mystery in their lives can be good. If a student knows that clandestinely writing-in wrong accidentals on the principal trumpet player's music will result only in a detention, they may decide it's worth it to see that show. That's way too much information in my opinion.

Our Attitude. Have you ever gotten a chip on your shoulder which started a negative chain reaction of attitudes? I have, and I always regret it. A student behaves badly, so we muster a nasty tone of voice and a firm reprimand, he gets worse, we get nastier, he then gets even worse and we get even nastier. And so it goes, an ever-deepening pit of negative attitudes, one feeding the other. It gets us nowhere. As the words of Buddha tell us, "Holding on to anger is like grasping a hot coal with the intent of throwing it at someone else; you are the one getting burned."

That scenario perfectly describes a situation I had many years ago when I first started teaching. I had this student whose attitude was awful from the day we met. In rehearsals he was almost combative. We started that war of who could have the worst attitude and it went on for weeks. After rehearsal one day, I called him into my office with the purpose of throwing him out of the ensemble. Before I did, however, I asked him why he behaved as he did. With as much anger as sadness in his voice, the young man went on to tell me about his recent attempt at suicide.

I sat there speechless, now listening to him rather than reprimanding him. Instantly, *my* attitude toward him changed from aggressive to supportive, angry to worried, antagonistic to caring. I went back to being a teacher. I wanted to help him change his attitude and behavior so he could experience joy, not only in my class, but in his life. Now in rehearsals when I have a student like that, I remember to be a teacher first and live the words of Jesse Jackson who warned, "Never look down on anyone unless you are helping them up."

It all comes down to one remarkable statement. Words that are as true when we are being negative, discouraging and disdainful as when we are being positive, encouraging and uplifting. Words by Dennis and Wendy Mannering that are at the core of being a teacher: "Attitudes are contagious. Are yours worth catching?" The answer to that question—for us and our students—may be as important as anything we teach.

Reinforcing Negative Behavior

Some of the most common responses to poor behavior take the form of *reinforcing negative behavior*. That's when poorly-behaved students get attention from you or other students for bad conduct. We catch them doing something wrong and then "reward" that action by letting them know they "got to us," or that they can derail our teaching. In that way, we prove they control the class by "pushing our buttons," and by so doing we *reinforce* that very behavior. What follows are the four most common ways we reinforce negative behaviors.

Shouting. Yelling only fuels the fire of an ever-escalating volume contest between teacher and students. We yell, they yell louder, so we yell still louder, and on it goes. And where it ends is always bad. It is antithetic to education, art, compassion and positive communication. It sidetracks real teaching, severely limits the manner in which the teacher speaks, and often ends up being the norm for classroom dialogue. Every time I hear a teacher yelling at his or her class I am reminded of the astoundingly astute words of Dagobert Runes: "You cannot train a horse with shouts and expect it to obey a whisper."

Threatening. We all know this is a lose-lose proposition, but it still rears its ugly head all too often. Making a threat to a misbehaving student is like waving a red flag in front of a bull; he has no choice but to "call us on it" just to test us. We have challenged him as if we had thrown down the proverbial gauntlet. Then we have either to make good on our threat, which is all too often something we regret having threatened, or back down and look powerless. Usually the student wins: game, set and match.

Fear and Sarcasm. Many of us lived through the days when this was the way it was done. A conductor ruled by fear and sarcasm. Fortunately, those days are gone. When used, fear and sarcasm only serve to let our students know they "got to us": wrecking our mood, ruining our flow, interrupting the music, and hijacking our rehearsal.

Punishment. I'm not a big believer in punishment. Do I use it? Yes, but I hate it because it proves to me that *I* failed: I had to resort to punishment because I couldn't find positive ways to solve the problem earlier. I let it become this bad. I didn't take positive steps to improve the situation, so now I am left with few choices. If I had just taken the "daily vitamins" of proactivity, I may have prevented the "disease" of bad behavior now confronting me.

All I know is if we use punishment, it must be done sparingly, carefully and dispassionately. The reason I dislike punishment stems from the fact that punishment may make students *stop the bad behavior*, but it won't make them *want to do the good behavior*.

If you feel you have dug yourself into a hole with these negative approaches, I would go with the advice of Molly Ivins who said, "The first rule of holes: When you're in one, stop digging." Yelling, threatening, sarcasm and punishment often just dig a deeper hole. Benjamin Hoff, when describing the Wu Wei principle of Tai Chi in his wonderful book, *The Tao of Pooh*, illustrates the problem as well as its solution when he writes, "The Wu Wei principle underlying Tai Chi can be understood by striking at a piece of cork floating in water. The harder you hit it, the more it yields; the more it yields, the harder it bounces back. Without expending any energy, the cork can easily wear you out. So, Wu Wei overcomes force by neutralizing its power, rather than by adding to the conflict. With other approaches, you fight fire with fire, but with Wu Wei, you fight fire with water."

We must remove the causes of poor behavior, not fight them. We must offer reasons for students to behave, as well as penalties when they don't. We must instill in them the desire to be part of the progress of the ensemble, not to be its impediment. We must remember it is far more productive to reward the good than to punish the bad. Even if our negative reactions do work, their effects are short-lived and usually foster negative feelings of hate, anger and embarrassment rather than positive feelings of cooperation, inspiration and striving for growth. So often, after a student has been dealt with negatively, I am left thinking, "Well, if he wasn't a real discipline problem before, he sure will be now!" So, if at first we don't succeed, let's find a different way.

Proactive Techniques and Approaches

What follows are proactive techniques and approaches—more positive ways—for controlling and disciplining students, improving behavior in rehearsals and inspiring motivation.

Reinforcing Positive Behavior. If it's true all we want is praise, encouragement, recognition—that "pat on the back" for success and completion, or trying and making progress—there is really only one path to take. The only approach to discipline that is long-term, long-lasting, self-disciplining, proactive, transferable, positively stimulating and uplifting is *reinforcing positive behavior.* Basically, catching students doing something good, praising those positive, wanted behaviors and desired actions, thereby causing an increase in the good behaviors, no matter what they may be: not playing on, a beautiful *crescendo,* a great release, marking a part, wonderful posture or improved hand position. It's simple: "If one person can say something to make someone feel bad, then maybe another person can say something to make him feel good." Praise encourages good behavior by making the student feel the benefits and rewards of *that* behavior. Reinforcing positive behavior keeps well-behaved kids behaving well, and makes poorly behaved kids behave better.

If needed, I'll "rig" events or stretch the truth a bit to creatively manufacture situations in order that students experience positive attention, so they taste the praise they've craved all along. But most importantly, we must remember to praise approximation: to applaud the steps along the way to the goal, no matter how small they may be. We can't wait to praise perfection (for that doesn't exist) or completion (for we may not live that long).

Some say too much praise is a bad thing. Let me ask you a question: do you ever get tired of hearing compliments about how good a teacher you are? Probably not. Now, if the praise is insincere, "over the top," ridiculously lavish, given when not deserved or doled out as if every time a group plays it achieves perfection, the purpose and power of the praise is diluted. But small doses of subtle recognition are all that is needed: a "thumbs up," a smile, a nod of the head, an okay sign or a few words of praise.

That said, care does need to be given with older students, especially those of high school age. Though praise for sections of the ensemble or the entire ensemble is perfectly fine, we do need to guard against praise which is too overt, or too much praise for single individuals, so they don't get branded a teacher's pet. Again, judicious care, subtlety and spreading the wealth of positive comments around the ensemble may remove any problem.

The Never-Ending Circle of Growth. Whatever the opposite of a vicious circle is, this is it. To me, it represents teaching at its best: linking reinforcement of positive behaviors to constructive criticism. It is best summed up in the words of President Dwight D. Eisenhower when he defined leadership as "the art of getting someone else to do something you want done because he wants to do it." This is where we praise, and thus reinforce, something a student is doing well to reward her success and bolster her self-esteem. Then immediately follow with one bit of constructive criticism which identifies something that needs improvement, offering specific comments on what to do to improve. Students feed on the positive comment, but at the same time know what to do to improve.

With comments such as, "Nancy, your posture is wonderful; now let's remember to keep our fingers closer to the keys," the never-ending circle of growth begins. The trick is for the little person on your shoulder—you know, the miniature you that sits there and serves as your eyes, ears, conscience, guide and filter—to go to work. His job now, while you are busy rehearsing the ensemble, is to stare at Nancy, just waiting for her to get her fingers closer to the keys so you can praise that success and offer new constructive criticism. The little man on your shoulder remembers so you can offer reinforcement at the first sign of improvement. With each pass of the circle, each nod of our praise and suggestion for improvement, we foster growth which is as uplifting as it is successful.

It does take an enormous amount of time to support every single student in this way. And though we can sometimes "get them" in groups, or as a whole ensemble, often it is done one student at a time. But getting, converting and keeping every student on the right path is worth every minute.

Your Personality. Have you ever stood in the customer service line at a store waiting to return a product that was a few days past the "return by" date? Watching the clerks assist each customer ahead of you, didn't you pick out the one who seemed the easiest mark and secretly hope you got him? Didn't you decide the person at counter number one was someone you wouldn't want to cross but the person at counter number eight seemed a soft touch? Well, students who are bent on misbehaving to get attention make those same decisions. We each need to develop a personality they won't want to cross or challenge, a personality so strong and intense they decide it's just not worth "messing with" or "trying you." Sad to say, but in their minds an easier mark may be found in the next class.

Draw Them In. Though I describe this in the chapter entitled *Draw Them to You*, the more positive goal of the previous entry is to use that intense persona—that *power of personality*—to capture the hearts and minds of our students. Through that ability, we can focus their energy, strengthen their concentration and empower their resolve. Call it mesmerizing, evangelical, compelling or charismatic; it can be the means by which we not only control a *group of people*, but facilitate an *ensemble* that is greater than the sum of its parts.

Start Firm. When I first started teaching, it was suggested to me that I begin every rehearsal firmly to settle the group, then once all is going well, relax the reins as the period goes on. Certainly, that isn't the only way, but it surely does seem to be the most secure and reliable way. We can always loosen our control, but it's very difficult for many to tighten it. The same advice holds true on a grand scale for the entire school year. I'm not talking about Dr. Jekyll morphing into Mr. Hyde but just a bit firmer start can make a huge difference.

Be Consistent. Essential to achieving a controlled environment is a teacher who is consistent from student to student and day to day. We must be consistent when dealing with our "best" students or our "far-from-best" students, when we are in a good mood or in a bad mood, and when confronted by the same behavior from different people. Consistency breeds standards and expectations; inconsistency breeds contempt.

Act Not React. When a teacher is confronted with a behavior problem, *reacting* to the situation—that knee-jerk response—almost always ends badly, reminding me of the prophetic words of Publius Syrus: "I have often regretted my speech, never my silence."

Taking a moment to think, then calmly *acting* upon that same situation, however, leads to a concerted, reasoned, thought-out, dispassionate response. That course of action almost always ends well. We just need to remember the words of the Chinese Proverb: "If you are patient in one moment of anger, you will escape a hundred days of sorrow." How many times in my life have I remembered those words ten minutes *too late* and lived to regret it?

Defuse First. Figuring out what caused a discipline problem is important, but as it is happening, it is far more important to defuse or stop it in its tracks. Analysis of what happened, thoughts of who was culpable and reflection about what *we* could have done better—more proactively—to prevent the problem, need to wait. We must put out the fire, then figure out what happened.

Show Interest. Showing interest and concern—making it a point to say something positive to every student as often as possible—is one of the most proactive ways to inspire them. Even a simple "How's everything?" or "Great job in chorus today!" as you pass them in the hall is good. Even better is when we can say something more personal, especially about their interests outside of music, such as, "How's your cold?" or "How was your baseball game?" To that end, at the start of the year, have students fill out information cards that include their interests. They can be incredibly helpful, especially for younger students.

It is difficult. It can challenge even the best memory of the most caring teacher. But it matters. Why? Because from a behavior standpoint, it's hard for a student to be a "rat" to someone who takes an interest in him. And from the human standpoint, it matters so much in the life of a child, a life we make better with every passing word.

Balance. I often worry that I dwell on the negative. Think of it: much of our job is assessing errors, finding what's wrong and deciding what needs to be fixed. In some ways, we are professional nitpickers. It's not that we are pessimists, but rather sometimes we use so much energy and concentration finding problems that we forget to balance our thoughts and—even more—our comments. So, years ago, I promised myself I would try to say something positive for every negative. I don't always succeed, but it does help me to remember that every half empty glass is also half full.

Use Necessary Repetition. Repetition is certainly part of what we do. I sometimes think clever, disguised ways of saying "play that again" make up a large part of a music teacher's vocabulary. And though sometimes we could target our teaching to reduce the amount, frequent repetition is necessary for reviewing material that has been learned, practicing techniques, putting what's been isolated back in context, and reinforcing basic concepts.

I think we should use those necessary repetitions as opportunities to praise. Each repetition gives us the chance to reinforce positive behaviors in our stellar students so they don't get bored, and link reinforcement of positive behaviors to constructive criticism for those needing more dramatic improvement. Since we're going to repeat something anyway, why not make the most of it?

Notes Home. During my junior year in college, I was given a very large solo in a piece with the wind ensemble. Though the composition had many smaller solos, mine was quite daunting. I don't think I've ever worked harder on anything in my life. The night of the performance came. I guess the fates were with me and the planets aligned correctly; I played it pretty well. Or so I thought. During the applause at the end of the work, the conductor had every soloist stand but me. You could hear a hushed gasp from the ensemble as it became clear I was not to be recognized. I was devastated. I remember walking back to the dorms replaying my performance over and over, wondering what was so bad as to offend my conductor. I had no answer, but I felt terrible.

The next morning I arrived at school quite early, and as usual, checked my mailbox. There I found a letter from my conductor. He apologized profusely for forgetting to have me stand. He went on to explain that he was going to have all the other soloists rise, then have me stand at the end, but in his worry about not forgetting anyone, he forgot me. But of far greater significance, he wrote about being proud of my effort and accomplishment. Isn't that amazing? In the real scope of things, it was a stupid little solo. However, to him—a real teacher—it meant much more.

You know what? I still have that letter somewhere up in my attic, and though I can't really tell you what it said, I will never forget how it made me feel. Now, all these years later, I think of him every time I write a note to a student or parent. If you haven't done it, try it; you will become addicted to the smile each note brings and the growth it encourages. Though I prefer to write, because then I control the amount of time I spend, some like to use the telephone. Either way, simply receiving "good news" from school will shock students and parents as much as delight them. And *after* Mr. and Mrs. Jones receive your letter or phone call praising their daughter Sue for her great work on posture and hand position, the conversation at home will go something like this:

"Susan, get in here!"
"What?"
"We just got this letter from your band teacher."
"Oh no, did I kill someone?"
"No, it said something about hands and position, and that he was proud of you. And so are we."

Those are moments that can change and shape lives, last a lifetime and represent teaching at its best. And every time you send a note home about a student's progress, improvement or success you do far more than make someone's day: you help make someone's life. They *may* forget what you said, but I'm here to tell you, they will *never* forget how you made them feel.

So promise yourself to send three notes home this week, but realize you will get addicted. It will start with three, and then six, then ten and before you know it you'll be hooked; not to the writing, but to the faces of the students whose lives you affect. Remember, you promised.

Engage Them. A student who is truly engaged in a rehearsal is unlikely to behave poorly. However, if a student is not engaged in the process he will be idle, bored or frustrated. At best, he will not be learning; at worst, he will become the source of behavior problems. Neither is acceptable.

We need to communicate with students by giving them something meaningful to watch with our faces and conducting. And by giving them something meaningful to hear, not only in the music, but from our comments of praise, information and constructive criticism. Something as simple as looking right in the eyes of every member of the ensemble before starting a rehearsal sets the expectation of mutual communication; even better, it sends a clear message about the importance of every student.

Stop Discipline Cells. Sixty kids don't all decide to misbehave at once. They just don't. It starts with one or two students in one spot and one or two in another spot. And then it spreads from there like a virus. The trick for us is to be so observant, sensitive and on top of what's happening in our environment that we prevent discipline cells from forming, and stop those that do form the second they start—before they can spread to other students or get out of hand. No advice is better than Mike Leavitt's, "There is a time in the life of every problem when it is big enough to see, yet small enough to solve."

Nonverbal Discipline. When it comes to controlling an ensemble with words, less is good, none is better. We can't underestimate the power of nonverbal discipline. Just *standing in silence*, glaring at students who misbehave is far more potent and compelling than just about anything we can say. When we speak, all too often we diminish the power of our personality, and "let them win" by confirming they "got to us."

Though that unadorned stare is usually persuasive enough, we can add a simple shaking of the head from side to side as if saying "no," or the pointing of an index finger with outstretched arm. Offering a look of disappointment can also be very effective; sometimes, depending on the student, far better than a look of anger. Some years ago, after a rehearsal where I looked at a certain section disappointedly, a student said to me, "In the future, would you just yell at us? It's far easier to take than when you look disappointed." That taught me a lot.

Walking over and standing in front of students who are disruptive can be very effective. If you are dealing with a very disruptive ensemble, you may even decide to add aisles through the group to facilitate getting near anyone. By making three or four small paths of space from your podium, out like radii all the way to the back of the group, you will gain the ability to stand near any disruptive student when needed. In addition, those different vantage points may offer better insights as to how each student is playing and make giving individual corrections more workable.

Silent Rehearsals. Although I have discussed silent rehearsals elsewhere in this book and in my previous book, *Teaching Music with Passion*, I mention it again because of its remarkable effectiveness. Nothing I know works better to focus an ensemble than posting the order of what will be played on the board, then having the conductor begin without so much as a word. Rehearsing with a conductor who is silent sets the tone and expectation of intense concentration, and creates an atmosphere of deafening quiet that students are unlikely to breach.

A Person of Few Words. Though silence may work best to control disruptive students, when we do choose to speak, being a man or woman of few words is almost always better than being the author of a long-worded, passionate reprimand. Short, pointed, powerfully calm statements to students who are behaving poorly, such as "No," or "Not again," work extremely well.

Fear of the Unknown. Looking directly at a student and emotionlessly saying, "I wouldn't do that again if I were you," is an example of this. It is *not* making a threat, but rather allows a student's imagination to concoct possibilities far worse than any reality we would threaten. The worry of not knowing the "what" of the teacher's statement makes the alternative of behaving well a more appealingly certain outcome.

Be Schizophrenic. Though it may sound crazy (sorry, I couldn't resist the pun!), this is where we go from our normal, vivacious, enthusiastic self, to disciplining a student with something like a cold, silent stare or terse "not again." But then we jump back to rehearsing the ensemble—on task and happy—even more musically excited, carefree and cheerful than before the interruption. Students come to understand they can't derail our plans, push our buttons or ruin our demeanor; quite frankly, it offers little reward and takes the purpose out of misbehaving.

Why?

What's this all about? What are we trying to inspire our students for? Is it really that important? You know the answers to those questions; all music teachers do, that's why we are who and what we are. But I'd like to share a story with you that helped me come to understand it so much better. A few years ago I attended the spring concert of a former student of mine. At the end of the concert, as was the tradition at this high school, the seniors in the band came to the front of the stage to give their director a gift. It was a pole, a metal pole. All I could think was, "Nice gift?!"

But in the back of the crowd of seniors, I could see two students holding something large, wrapped in a blanket. After the puzzled audience—and band director—had a moment to digest the idea of a metal pole as a gift, those two students made their way to the front of the stage. With almost solemn dignity, they unveiled a sign. It was a metal street sign to be affixed to that pole and placed in front of the school. It was a sign for the reserved parking space they somehow finagled for their band director. Now I don't know about where you teach, but where I teach, a parking space is worth its weight in platinum.

Then the seniors spoke about their four years with the ensemble and their teacher. No one spoke of how many running sixteenth-notes they played cleanly, how many trophies they won, how many grade six pieces they performed, or the results achieved at state contest. Instead, they spoke of how their teacher and this ensemble changed their lives, helped them become better people, gave them eyes to see the beauty in the world, and made them able to feel emotions as they walked through life. That's what it's all about. That's why it's so important. Because our students, just like us, don't remember the black dots on a page, they remember feelings. Not just from our telling them what to do, but by our inspiring them to do it.

How?

But how do we inspire? Well, I have a little formula: "I = C + P + E." It's easy to remember; I just think of Carl Philipp Emanuel Bach. "I," inspiration, equals "C," curiosity: for learning, for what's on the next mountaintop, for what's possible. Plus "P," praise: for the steps along the way, for beauty, for trying, for effort. Plus "E," emotion: for the chills, the tingles up the spine, the tears, the tapping into one's soul. That's inspiration.

I bet you're wondering why there was no mention of an "E" for enjoyment. I believe enjoyment is important, but I also believe it is a byproduct of being inspired through curiosity for what we can be, praise for what we are, and feeling the emotions of what we create.

How do we inspire? A sentiment borrowed from Socrates says it best: Excite me and I will learn anything, make me curious and I will learn even more. Our enthusiasm must excite our students to be curious, to want to learn, to explore, to try, to follow, and to *learn* that *learning* itself is amazing. If our rehearsals are controlled, we can train our students. Then teach them and inspire them. Then watch them motivate themselves, and grow, and flourish, and cry, and be sad, and feel joy and all manner of emotions.

We will have given them the greatest gift imaginable: the appreciation of themselves and life. We will have taught them to feel, and truly to understand the words of Leonard Bernstein when he wrote, "Music can name the unnamable and communicate the unknowable." And we will have taught them to aspire, and to live the words: "Go as far as you can see, and when you get there, you'll see farther."

I'd like to ask you a question. If the moment you started reading this chapter I placed a small white box on a table in front of you with no words of explanation, would you, by the end of the chapter, be wondering what was in it? And as the minutes passed, if I kept turning and moving it around the table, would your wondering turn to puzzlement? If then I intermittently stuck flashing lights of different colors, shapes and sizes on the box to continually draw your attention to the box, would you become curious? When I present this chapter as a session for conferences that is exactly what I do.

At the end of the session, I simply put the box back in my briefcase with no words of explanation. Most often, that action is accompanied by an audible groan from all present, and quasi-angry questions about what was in the box. My answer is always the same: "Oh, the box. Are you *curious* about what's in the box? I think Socrates would have liked that!"

I then open the box, revealing nothing but a worthless, crumpled-up, empty candy wrapper. After people settle in to their disappointment, I look inside the wrapper, and show to all a brand new $100 bill. Things aren't always as they seem. It's not what our students are; it's what they can become. Every child must be taught to reach for the stars. Every child can learn and become anything, if *we* help them to bring it out.

No one taught me this better than my mother. You see, my mom was a wonderful artist, as talented as she was humble. She had a studio in the basement of our home, and on the wall next to her easel hung a very small frame which my dad made for her. In the frame was a small piece of paper onto which she copied the following words, elegantly adorning them with a flowering vine. They are from a letter of introduction from patron to pope which reads:

The bearer of these presents is Michelangelo, the sculptor. His nature is such that he requires to be drawn out by kindness and encouragement. But, if love be shown him and he is well treated, he will accomplish things that will make the whole world wonder.

Who knows what student, even those that may seem like crumpled-up candy wrappers, may, with love and encouragement, "...accomplish things that will make the whole world wonder"?

PERCUSSIONISTS: THE MISSING "PEACE"?

Here we are in the middle of a seventh-grade band rehearsal: ninety students focusing every ounce of concentration on their conductor and the music they are making. All, that is, but the eight percussionists not playing this composition, who are sitting in the back of the room. There they are sitting in a row of chairs placed just to the back of the ensemble. In a perfect world, they would be jotting down the score in dictation, followed by a complete Schenkerian analysis and detailed notes on historically accurate performance practice. However, that would be in a perfect world. Here, we see them plotting, lurking in the shadows of our rehearsal. Sometimes they are staring right at us as if to be on lookout, while at other times they disappear down below the horizon of our view of the band, offering a sinister, all-too-suspicious look of pure evil. We often wonder *what* they're planning, not *if* they're planning. As we work with the rest of the ensemble, fear and trepidation distracts us.

Though undoubtedly I am overstating this problem to the extreme, if you have ever lived through it, you may think I am not being pessimistic enough. Over the years, I have heard stories about those "extra" percussionists, ranging from their setting fire to a pile of costumes during a rehearsal on an auditorium stage, to their letting loose a stink bomb in the middle of a Sousa march. While those do represent the worst examples of behavior, they nonetheless illustrate a problem. Even if those percussionists were models of good behavior, the essence of the problem still exists: a lack of *time on task*.

What do percussionists do during those long stretches of boredom? The most respectful of them may do homework for another class, or read a book, or actually attend to the rehearsal. However, it is possible they will attempt to get attention from you or from their peers by misbehaving. Assigning written work, silent reading or study sheets may occupy them, but rarely seems to work well. Putting them at desks scattered around the room may work, but often gives behavior-problem children a soapbox from which to broadcast. Certainly praising them for sitting quietly can go a long way toward reinforcing positive behavior, but negative attention given for poor behavior is an alluring temptation for some students.

Even if they are not practicing up on the latest techniques for disrupting a rehearsal, they are also not taking part in the educational process; at best, they are allowing that learning to happen all around them. During those times of sitting "on the bench" they are not getting much of an education. Look at it this way: you are a student in a math class. At the first meeting of the class, the teacher tells you there are not enough math books for the number of people in the class. Since each class period will be spent doing math problems from the book, which you often won't have, you are to sit in a chair in the back of the class and just watch the others do their work. And don't forget, during that time you will be expected to be a model of good behavior.

How long would it take you to misbehave? Doesn't that scene sound shockingly similar to the archaic "dunce sitting in the corner" technique of classroom discipline? Those students didn't do anything to warrant that treatment. They simply chose a very popular instrument. Am I saying all percussionists are by nature discipline problems or malicious? No! I am saying that if you take any small group of young people, put them in chairs in the back of an ensemble far away from the teacher and remove them from the task at hand, they will have the *potential* for very poor behavior. It is *certain*, however, they will be spending a great deal of time *not* on task. What is the solution? Have all twenty percussionists play each piece? Let them sit in the back and goof around? Neither.

The percussion section of an ensemble can undoubtedly be the very core of its spirit, power, finesse, precision and ability to paint a picture. Adding a good percussion section to an ensemble is like finding the missing piece of a puzzle. Without it, the picture couldn't be right. With it, vivid meaning comes alive. Sadly, a poorly behaved and poorly trained percussion section may become the *missing "peace"*: a source of disruptive behavior and less-than-educational activity. But how can we keep them *all* on task and train them to be the percussionists we need and want? How do we make a "bunch of drummers" into a "percussion section?" What follows are a few ideas.

Air Drums

Without question, sound recruiting efforts that limit the number of percussionists as part of securing balanced instrumentation is the best solution. Choosing music that has many percussion parts and includes a vast number of percussion instruments, as well as limiting (though certainly not excluding) the number of compositions performed that have few or no percussion parts, can also help. Still, we will often have far more performers than parts. This is where *air drums* come in. It's a technique I developed years ago, the positive aspects of which never cease to surprise me. In an effort to have every percussionist play as often as possible without creating so much volume as to be overwhelming, I suggest building or buying comparatively silent instruments to augment traditional instruments. This is simply the use of practice pads taken to the extreme.

Air snare drum or tenor drum parts can be played on traditional practice pads mounted on stands. Though I prefer the type made of rubber, which create less sound, any variety of drum pad will work. For timbale, roto-tom, multiple concert toms and the like, I use two or more pads set up as needed to imitate the arrangement of the traditional instruments.

Air bass drums can be made by stuffing an appropriate-sized cardboard box with newspaper, sealing it tightly, and covering the batter side with heavy-gauge plastic sheeting secured with duct tape. Air timpani can be made by using two or more of those cardboard-box drums. Air bass drums can be put on a bass drum stand or small desk. Air timpani can be put on a table or several desks.

An air xylophone can be made by cutting a piece of thin plywood or heavy cardboard to approximately the size and shape of the frame of that instrument. Cover that with a sheet of 3/8 inch white foam board on which you have drawn the keyboard of a xylophone. The trick is to make the drawing as realistic and accurate as possible. That should be covered with a sheet of heavy-gauge plastic secured with duct tape. The air xylophone can be placed on a table or a pair of sawhorses. Though I have found air orchestra bells and air xylophone work best, air marimba and air vibes can be made the same way.

I would use air drums only for mallet and headed instruments, leaving all other percussion instruments to be played by one player on traditional instruments. I have, however, heard of some teachers of young students using air crash cymbals made of cardboard with cloth straps, air suspended cymbals made of cardboard on a stand and air triangles made of cloth-covered coat hangers bent into that shape. Whether you want to go to those extremes, or simply use additional snare players on pads, the point is to get every percussionist playing as often as possible.

Let's say we have a piece that calls for timpani, bass drum, crash cymbals, triangle, snare drum, orchestra bells and xylophone. Without doubling any part, we need seven players. But what do we do if we have fifteen percussionists? Double many parts with the concomitant clutter and volume that would create? No. We have those "other" eight players on task by including one air bass drum, two air orchestra bells, two air xylophones and two air snare drums. But how do we stage their placement? Who gets to play traditional versus silent instruments, and what do we do at the concert?

As to placement, I suggest setting up the traditional percussion instruments as you like. Then place each air instrument slightly behind and to the side of the traditional player, creating diagonal rows going away from the conductor. For each composition, students are assigned to a part. For parts being played by more than one player, which employ both traditional and air drums, students randomly stand at either the air drum or real instrument. At which of those they start doesn't matter.

During the course of rehearsing that piece, or, if you prefer, from one rehearsal to the next, you simply say "switch." That is their signal to rotate through their diagonal row of air drums and traditional instruments. The beauty is they can do this task virtually instantaneously since they will each have sticks or mallets in hand, and the instruments (or air drums), music stands and music will already be in place. They simply move from one spot to the next. I suggest using the air drums, as described above, in all rehearsals leading up to the concert.

As to the concert, just prior to the event, post a listing of permanent assignments for the performance, making certain each student plays some of the time on traditional instruments. But let's face it: parents in the audience will note how *often* their children are playing, more than on *what* they are playing. The bottom line is that all the percussionists are *on task* and truly engaged in rehearsals.

Adding Parts

One solution some conductors use to solve the problem of an abundant number of percussionists is to add percussion parts to a composition. This is done by doubling parts written for one percussion instrument to other percussion instruments, having mallet instruments double existing wind instrument parts, or simply by writing new percussion parts for the work. Certainly, where the composer gives license for "ad lib" parts, the sky is the limit. As well, certain styles or periods of music may lend themselves to some judicious additions. More than that, absent supportive correspondence from the composer, I think air drums are a far better option.

Warm-Ups

If we have too many percussionists, and they become a source of concern because they are not engaged in the rehearsal or spending enough time on task, when is it that they go astray? When do we lose them? More often than not, it's during the warm-up portion of our rehearsal, especially if that is an extended period of time spent working on exercises which exclude percussionists.

So we need to engage them in that portion of rehearsal as well. But how?

They certainly can play any warm-up material using air mallets. Or we could write out parts to be played on air drums so students can practice rudiments or faster complex rhythmic exercises while the rest of the ensemble plays chordal passages or scales in slow-moving whole tones.

Another approach that works very well, though difficult to implement, is having the percussion section move to a different room or practice room which is set up with practice pads or air drums for the warm-up portion of the rehearsal. This can only work if that extra room exists and if there is another teacher that can go with those students. As complicated as that may sound, this works especially well in situations that use team teaching or teacher/support-teacher concepts. However, even absent those, it can work. How about making a deal with another teacher to help him in his class during the first few minutes of your prep period, if he helps you in band during the first few minutes of his prep period? How great would it be for the band director to help with the tuning process for the beginning string orchestra during the first seven minutes of that rehearsal, if the orchestra director runs the percussion warm-up for the first seven minutes of band? Depending on schedules it may be impossible, but creative thinking may result in a wonderful solution.

If we don't, won't or can't find a way to improve time-on-task opportunities for our percussionists during rehearsal warm-up sessions, staying keenly aware of the amount of time *that* portion of rehearsal uses is key. Forty-minute band rehearsals that start with twenty minutes of tuning and warming-up, where percussionists play little or nothing, at best are an educational weakness and at worst can ignite enormous behavior problems.

Chairs

We have all seen it: the gang of percussionists seated in the back of an ensemble. Dutifully they wait for their turn to play something, anything: a snare drum, a cymbal, Steve's head. There they sit, patiently at first, but as time goes on they grow fidgety. Fidgety then turns to antsy. Antsy turns to disruptive. Though air drums, and the like, undoubtedly will reduce the amount of down time for these students, there *will be* down time. The trick is to limit that time the same way we would limit the time during which only the clarinets play in a rehearsal so as not to bore the rest of the ensemble. As conductors, we are always on guard for balancing time with one section, giving it the attention it needs, with the fact the rest of the ensemble is growing bored and anxious. Undoubtedly, we must train young percussionists to remain focused and quiet during times they do not play, as long as we ensure those times are appropriate in duration and frequency.

But what about *where* they are when they're not playing? Go back to the above-mentioned scene. There they *sit* behind the ensemble: partially obscured from view, only visible from the head up. Isn't that a recipe for mutiny and chaos? Those chairs almost take them away from sight *and* from the ensemble. Why are chairs needed? The typical rehearsal just isn't that long. Do students sit during gym class? In addition, we will now have them on task so much of the time they will not find it as necessary, or possible, to sit. I advocate getting rid of the chairs completely, eliminating one more potential source of trouble. With those chairs removed, I am able to see every percussionist, am able to sense when they are losing interest, and, most importantly, am better able to keep them engaged and truly part of the rehearsal. We would never coach the basketball team by sending some of our players to sit in the farthest bleachers, would we? If you truly feel the need for chairs, or if you rehearse as part of a long block schedule where it becomes necessary, then I suggest having the chairs along the side, toward the front of the ensemble. Or, place a few chairs for them at the end of each row of the rest of the ensemble. In that way, on the outside of the row of first violins in the orchestra or third clarinets in the band, the percussionists are in plain sight and easily managed.

Treat Them Like Musicians

I know those words sound harsh, but so often percussionists complain they are treated like second-class citizens in ensembles. I guess we are all guilty of sometimes concentrating so much on the winds and strings that it may seem that way *to percussionists*. It goes far beyond simply paying attention to them. We must be as critical and exacting with their playing as we are with other sections. We must treat them as "musically" as we do other players, discussing and attending to attacks, releases and musical aspects of their playing no differently than those of the flutes and clarinets. We must be as demanding with their playing position and technique as we are with those of the violins and violas, attending to physical attributes of holding and playing each instrument: grip for, and choice of, sticks, mallets and beaters; choice of size and timbre of cymbals and triangles; and the like.

We must ask them for their musical judgments and guide them in making decisions that are musically and technically sound. We can draw them into the rehearsal by asking them to decide when they are dominant or supportive, structural or simply providing color. Put simply, we must treat them as musicians and demand from them the same exacting attention to detail we would any

other section of the ensemble. The truth be known, with the myriad of instruments and techniques with which they must be profi-
cient, they need and deserve all the attention we can give them.

To that end, we need to get them all the instruments called for
at any given time. Not only is it what the music demands, it is part
of our percussionists' training and education. What message does
it send a young percussionist who is told to play the finger cymbal
part on the triangle, or the vibraslap on the woodblock, or the
wind chimes on the tambourine? It is as wrong musically as it is
pedagogically, and leads a percussionist to feel that he or she, and
that part, is unimportant. As one of my percussionists once said to
me, "We like you because you buy us all the toys we need!" Sometimes, those "toys" make all the difference in the world in the life
of a composition and the players entrusted to perform it.

Make Them Play Everything

In keeping with the above statements, shouldn't we teach percussionists to play all the standard members of the percussion family?
How sad it is to see a young person who possesses great skill on
the snare drum, but is incapable of tuning timpani or playing a
scale on the xylophone. Certainly students will have strengths
and weaknesses, but we cannot allow our students to stunt their
growth by only focusing on one area of their education.

How to Start?

Without a doubt, starting beginning percussionists on only the
snare drum contributes to the problem. Starting them on only
mallet instruments or mallets *and* snare drum, however, seems to
limit enrollment to more serious percussionists, and gives them

a jump start on a well-rounded percussion education. Though concerns arise about the number of available instruments (solved in great measure by the use of air drums), and the demands of the music for the first concert, you may decide the positives far outweigh the negatives.

Another method I have seen work very well is to start percussion lessons in the *second* year of the elementary program, allowing students to switch to percussion only after having at least one year on another band or orchestra instrument. In districts where this is the established norm, it causes no conflict: it just is. Moving to this policy where it does not exist will probably stir up controversy at first, but depending on how bad your situation is, you may decide it's worth the fight.

The Bottom Line

Picture the all-too-common situation of a percussionist being told she will play only one of the pieces the band will be working on for the next three months. And, even though the part calls for triangle, wind chimes, finger cymbals and bell tree—since the school owns only the triangle—she is to play all of those parts on the triangle. Now, wouldn't that be the same as saying to an oboe player that he will play only one of the pieces the band will be rehearsing for the next three months, and since we don't own an oboe with a C-sharp key, he should just play all those C-sharps as C-naturals? It *is* the exact same situation, but no one would ever allow the latter to happen.

We all know percussionists can be the heart and soul of an ensemble when attended to appropriately. When given the training and attention they deserve they can be the sparkle that makes a group shine, the foundation that makes it solid and the power that makes it majestic. However, they, like any other section, when allowed to disengage from a rehearsal truly can become the missing "peace." Let us resolve to have *every* percussionist feel as though he or she is as important to the ensemble as the principal flute. It will make all the difference in the world. ■

DRAW THEM TO YOU

It never ceases to amaze me: the whole notion of one lone person—a conductor—standing in front of large numbers of people single-handedly guiding them. Not just guiding, but leading them; getting all of them to yield their individual opinions to that of the conductor. Think about it for a minute. Isn't it astounding when it works? Yet sadly, when it doesn't work, it reminds me of the old joke: "Watching a conductor, it's often hard to tell if he's leading a group or running from a mob." Indeed.

When watching a master teacher or conductor, however, words like commanding, authoritative, magnetic, mesmerizing and confident spring to mind. With the days of fear and intimidation, fortunately, well behind us, great leaders simply are able to bring each member of the ensemble to them, becoming a compelling focal point for the members' individual and collective eyes, ears and minds.

Whether we want to improve discipline, have more intense rehearsals, better train an ensemble to watch or be a more powerful communicative presence, we must be like a vortex pulling students toward us, a whirlpool focusing their concentration on us, a vacuum drawing them to us, and a magnet attracting their every sense to us. Like the "tractor-beam" in a *Star Wars* movie leaves no other choice for its prey than to be pulled toward the source, we need to create a con-

nection strong enough to capture every student's attention. I think
we do this in three ways: psychologically, aurally and physically.

Psychologically

To me, the *power of our personality* is the single most important factor in becoming that focal point, in getting our students to listen
to, and watch us, intensely. Some people call it a "magnetic personality," others "charisma," but whatever you call it, the power of
a personality can be gripping, compelling and spellbinding. With
equal parts confidence, passion, sincerity, concern, enthusiasm,
knowledge and intensity, a powerful personality can move mountains. Developing that rich, powerful personality is essential for
drawing them in; it is also invigorating by its contagious nature.

Every teacher's powerful personality certainly will be different, featuring aspects of his or her natural disposition, but we
each can be that *powerful personality* in our own way, drawing every
student's mind and psyche to ours.

Aurally and Physically

Picture this scene: it's Friday afternoon before a vacation, last period of the day (with the previous period having been a pep rally),
it just started snowing for the first time all season and you have a
rehearsal. Imagine the energy and adrenaline pulsing through the
core of every student in that room. Many teachers, in an effort to
"corral" the students into getting focused and settled, will start
that rehearsal using a thunderously loud voice, perhaps the loudest voice they use in that rehearsal. Why? The logic is that the
loud voice will "get the students' attention" and bring their focus
toward the teacher.

Similarly, in that situation teachers will often use their largest conducting gestures—those more suited to landing large aircraft—at the start of the rehearsal in an effort to get the ensemble to watch. In this case, those gestures are not chosen for expressive purposes, but out of a sense of perceived necessity or self-preservation.

Unfortunately, those giant physical and verbal actions, more often than not make the situation worse, not better. If the ensemble is chatty at the start of rehearsal and we begin with a loud voice, they just chat louder, then we talk even louder, and they follow suit. All our loud voice did was to escalate the volume frenzy, not remedy it. It is much like putting gasoline on a burning fire.

Likewise, starting an even somewhat unruly rehearsal with over-conducted gestures, in an effort to firmly take control and concentrate student attention on our conducting, begins the visual equivalent of that shouting match mentioned above. Those enormous gestures don't intensify our students' visual attention and precision; rather, they dilute and spread it. Then we conduct even larger gestures which diffuse their attention still more. And so goes the vicious cycle of ever-increasing gestures.

I think, however, when it comes to the use of our voice and gestures in rehearsals, we would be better—far better—served to remember the words of Martin Heidegger who wrote, "We pursue that which retreats from us." Using that wisdom, we can work to eliminate those escalating voice-volume and gesture-size power struggles by moving in the opposite direction of the examples above.

We simply can't physically or aurally reach out and "grab the attention" of sixty members of an ensemble. And even if we could, they would retreat from us. We can't lurch forward to connect with all of them at once, but we can draw them all to us at once. If we start with firm, modestly small-sized gestures and then gradually get *smaller* to focus our students, they will be forced to come to us. Gestures that steadily decrease in size do just that. Gradually shrinking gestures that compact our students' fields of vision force them toward us.

Similarly, if we start rehearsals with one or two firm and assertive words like "Good morning," or "Okay," then get softer with every word as we continue to speak, we will gradually capture our students' attention and aurally draw them toward us. In that way, using Heidegger's insight, we can "retreat" from them with our voice and conducting so they "pursue" us.

Once we have the eyes and ears of the ensemble and are the focal point of their attention, we can use our voice and gestures as we wish, knowing we can resort back to those smaller or softer versions if needed to regain our foothold.

Draw Them In

What follows are a few gimmicks I would like to suggest that are extraordinarily effective as we work toward the goal of drawing students in.

A Tired Horse. One of the tactics a trainer can use when breaking a horse is to use the horse's own natural vitality to tire it out. Rather than try to train the horse while it has incredible pent-up energy, that energy is intentionally expended in a controlled manner, making the horse more willing to yield to instruction. We can do the same thing. When students come to rehearsals "wired," we need to let them vent some of that energy, making them more willing to acquiesce. The trick is to allow them to get rid of that exuberance in a beneficial way.

At the start of a rehearsal in which I sense students are, shall we say, brimming over with boisterous enthusiasm (how's that for a euphemism?), I ask everyone, with no explanation or fanfare, to sing or play a very comfortable unison pitch or major triad as a long tone. I tell them and show with my conducting that I want it to be voluminously loud. Immediately, I start to show an incredibly slow, gradual decrescendo that seems to take forever.

I do this several times with only a quick breath in between, making each attack start a bit softer then the previous one started and end a bit softer than the previous one ended. In this way the first tone may go from *fff* to *mp*, then the next from *ff* to *p*, then *mf* to *pp* and *p* to *pppp*. As I do this, I gradually concentrate the focus of my eyes, staring at my hands as they move closer together in the students' shrinking fields of vision while using facial expressions that show severe concentration on my hands. As each sound moves softer in volume, our students' listening becomes sensitized to ever-softer sounds that intensify their concentration. Likewise, as our gestures draw smaller and closer to our sternum, our ensemble's vision becomes more powerfully focused on our every motion.

At the end of this exercise, in the deafening silence of the pregnant pause created after sensitively releasing the final *pianissimo* sound of the now reasonably tired, extraordinarily focused, extremely controlled ensemble, a soft word or two from the conductor sets the tone for continued concentration and focus. Not only will the students expend vast amounts of excess energy while unknowingly being drawn to you, the exercise is a wonderful opportunity to reinforce skills and concepts such as watching the conductor, posture, tone quality, breath support and dynamic control.

Something's Different. Sometimes something as simple as drastically changing the set-up of an ensemble can be enough to stimulate renewed focus on the conductor. Why it works, I don't know, but it really does work. One day have the students come into the rehearsal room only to find it set up in concentric circles with you in the center. Or, how about in a traditional set-up, but with many aisles added through the ensemble like radii from the podium.

Both of these set-ups, and a myriad of others, allow you to "shock" the students with something new, get eminently closer to each member of the ensemble and move around the ensemble with relative freedom. Each is extremely conducive to intensifying focus and concentration, as well as improving behavior and assessing individual student achievement and ability. It's amazing how something as simple and easy as changing an ensemble's set-up can pay so many dividends.

The Silent Conductor. As I have said before, a conductor's speech rarely serves to intensify student focus on the podium. Quite to the contrary, it usually scatters student concentration to the wind. With that in mind, a wonderfully effective way to draw students in is for the conductor to rehearse without making a sound, what I call a "silent rehearsal." One of my favorite techniques, this is where the students walk into the rehearsal room only to find the material for the day written on the board and the conductor standing at the podium in silence. By pointing to the board or holding up scores to indicate the composition, using fingers to show measure numbers and flashcards with letter names written on them for rehearsal letters, rehearsal takes place with total silence from the conductor.

Not only does the silence act to intensify concentration and focus on the conductor, and improve discipline, it forces the conductor to describe what he or she wants with only gestures and facial expressions. With the only stimulus being the conductor emulating sound in motion, words can no longer be relied on to shape the desired sounds. It basically forces us to "put our hands and face where our mouth is."

Tossing the Handkerchief. As said earlier, very large conducting gestures, when used for the purpose of "lassoing" student focus, usually fail. In fact, those gestures seem to do the opposite, diminishing the conductor as the focal point by "physically" scattering student concentration.

Starting rehearsals with relatively small gestures does help draw students in, but sometimes, when students are extremely unfocused, we may want an even more powerful tool. It is then that I remember back to my teenage years, when I watched many live performances of the wonderful trumpeter Maynard Ferguson. Often, while fronting his magnificent big band, Maynard would reach into his pocket and get a handkerchief. He would then entertain his spellbound audience by throwing the piece of cloth in the air, only to have the band strike a short, earth-shatteringly dramatic *sforzando* the split second the hankie hit his hand. It was so very impressive.

This would go on for quite some time, mesmerizing every member of the audience with the communicative power seemingly gathered in the handkerchief as it ascended, only to explode as it finished its descent. The intensity of this simple "gesture" was overwhelming in its control, precision and ability to focus every eye to even the smallest of motions. It was as captivating as it was communicative.

With Maynard's showmanship in mind, on those few occasions when I feel I need a bit of help drawing my students to me, I simply reach into my back pocket and grab my handkerchief. I crumble the hankie into a ball, tell the students to play one short, accented concert B-flat tone when they see the handkerchief hit my hand, and then throw the cloth in the air. It is amazing how well this works. The students become more fascinated with every throw of the handkerchief. To them, what may have begun as a "silly little game" takes on more and more communicative intensity, heightens focus on the conductor, and adds more to the challenge with every toss. Once they are focused on my hands, I simply return the hankie to my pocket and have them play the

same sound as I conduct normally, thereby transferring their concentration from the cloth to my hands.

For a twist on this gimmick, use a brightly colored tennis ball in
place of the handkerchief. With its more obvious and vivid deceleration as it ascends, and acceleration as it descends, it becomes even
easier for the students to "prepare" for every attack they play. In this
way, linking everyday experiences and activities to our conducting,
we help our students better understand, and sense, the function of
our hands and baton in every preparatory gesture we conduct.

Since we can control the manner and direction more accurately
when tossing the ball than when tossing the hankie, I like to use it
to prove to my students the communicative power of small, well-
prepared gestures by simply tossing the ball straight up in the air
two feet or more, having them play as before when the ball lands in
my hand. Then, little by little, I reduce the height of the toss so that
they finally play after a toss that rises up in the air no more than an
inch or so. They quickly will see that some of their best and most
assured attacks occur after the ball is tossed the shortest distance,
proving what makes this "work" is the power of the preparation gesture and the concentration of those who watch it, not its size.

Keeping Them Drawn In

Without question, drawing our students to us is an admirable goal;
however, *keeping* them focused, receptive and responsive is just as
important. Getting them to come to the table and taste the appetizer is the first step, but getting them to stay through dessert,
let alone to want to come back for future meals, must be our true
purpose. Ultimately, it is what our students see and hear from
us once we have their focus upon us that matters. It is the quality of our communication—especially that which is nonverbal in

nature—that keeps them focused on us and, more importantly, draws them in further and more intensely.

Providing conducting motions and gestures our students can predict and easily understand is vital to that goal. If students receive clear and meaningful communication from the conductor, they will be enticed and encouraged to watch for more. If what they see makes sense to them according to their intrinsic, experiential logic, it needs no explanation. They then can act upon that information, able to predict outcomes and reactions. Quite simply, that which is logical to us is meaningful, useful, engaging and inviting.

I have always held that if gestures, and our manner of motion, are rooted in the laws of science, they will be just that: understood and predictable. As long as movements agree with our knowledge and experience of physical motion, we can predict them without thought or effort. We have seen apples fall from trees since birth; does anyone need to have the inherent acceleration to the ground explained to him? We have watched stones skim on a pond, a pendulum swing from an axis, and balls bounce on the ground. Do any of those motions or actions need reasoned clarification? Of course not; we have lived with them all our lives. The same holds true for conducting.

To that end, when working with student conductors and a laboratory ensemble, I also use the tennis ball technique mentioned above to illustrate the value and power of several of those firmly held beliefs about conducting gestures and motion, namely: (1) Simple gestures always work better than fancy motions that performers must figure out; (2) even the smallest of gestures will work as long as the gesture is prepared; (3) beat motion does not move at a constant rate of speed, but rather shows deceleration *from* one beat and acceleration *to* the next beat, within the confines of the tempo, like a bouncing ball; and (4) all gestures must allow for reaction time necessary for performers to see the gesture, process what they are seeing, determine what to do and then execute the response.

For this, I simply ask the ensemble to play the same sort of attack when the ball touches the palm of my outstretched left hand as they had before. Then, instead of tossing the ball, I hold it in my right hand and move it around in large florid motions that flow at a constant speed. Continuing to move in this manner, with no acceleration or deceleration, I have the ball ultimately "arrive" in my left palm.

When one does this, the ensemble's attack is always sloppy because the "gesture" is confusing, does not allow for reaction time, and, absent acceleration and deceleration, makes the arrival difficult for performers to predict. I do this a few times, proving the point with each inaccurate attack. Finally, I toss the ball straight up in the air as before, with the result always being a far better, if not exceptional attack. This easily demonstrates that allowing for reaction time, harnessing a performer's ability to predict and anticipate gestures by use of motions that accelerate and decelerate—like those of a thrown ball rising and falling in the air—allows for preparatory gestures that are extraordinarily functional and causative.

Conclusion

Whether we seek to enhance our rapport with our performers, to strengthen our mutual communication, to further develop our abilities to control an ensemble, or to sustain an intensely vibrant rehearsal environment, the key is our ability to draw them to us physically, mentally and emotionally. Productive, indeed, are conductors who discover the treasure that awaits them once they accept the fact that our students will *pursue that which retreats from them.* Richer still are conductors who work to use that fact to the benefit of their students, the ensemble and the music.

The Parable of the
Tandoori Chicken

My three children love Indian food. For years, my bringing home Indian food for dinner has been one of their favorite treats. Being a creature of habit, on those occasions I would call our favorite Indian restaurant and have our order ready for me to pick up on my way home from the University. My order always starts the same way: "One order of Tandoori chicken, very well done with sautéed onions and green peppers, and mild sauce." This has always worked beautifully. I would pick up the order. I would arrive home and ceremoniously announce I brought home Indian food. It was cooked to perfection. Daddy was a hero!

But one day it all went horribly wrong. This time, when I called the restaurant, I noticed the employee that answered the phone spoke very little English. It turns out she was a new member of the staff and unlike everyone else there who spoke fluent English, she was just learning. When I picked up the order I was fearful, but optimistic. I drove home, made my announcement, and we all sat down to eat. However, this time the order was completely wrong. It was in every way *not* what we wanted: the wrong dish, cooked the opposite of how we wanted it and with a sauce so hot I believe it spontaneously combusted in one's mouth. One by one, my children showed their disappointment. Well shy of hero status, I wasn't sure I would be allowed to sleep in the house that night.

So I started complaining about that employee: how she messed up, how she didn't speak enough English to do her job and how we would now have to find a new Indian restaurant because of her, and on and on. I complained and moaned and griped until finally my wife, who had been silent while I vented, simply said: "Why don't you just learn to say the order in her language?"

I stopped dead in my tracks. Why didn't I think of that? I was so busy being angry with the problem that I never thought about a solution. Here was an opportunity for me to remedy a problem instead of complain about it. In addition, it was an opportunity for *me* to learn something. All I needed to do was to *use* those words of Henry Ford: "Don't find fault. Find a remedy!" With a little effort, I could have solved a problem and ended up smarter to boot.

When we are confronted by students who "can't get it" or we can't get them to "want to get it," do we complain about the situation, or do we take those moments as opportunities to be a better teacher? Do we take kids where they are, the way they are, and figure out how to teach them?

You know, I still can't walk into that restaurant without grinning. That employee made me a better teacher and a better student. Every day, I wonder how many of those opportunities I miss.

Let us all remember the wonderful Zen proverb that goes something like this: "Inside or outside yourself you never have to change what you see, only the way you see it." We must always be on the lookout for our next chance to teach, our next chance to learn, our next chance to be the best teacher we can be. ◾

"One Moment of Anger"

So, there I was, in the middle of a rehearsal with my University Band. We were working on a technically difficult passage of very fast, pointillistic *staccato* pitches that were being passed around the ensemble like gunfire. The problem was it sounded as if the players were all at the firing range wearing blindfolds! It was amazing to me that after ninety minutes of remarkable playing, this passage was getting the better of us. I did what any music teacher would do: I rehearsed that short section with determination. It got worse. So I tried doing it with a very intense, dogmatic drive that surely should have focused their concentration. It got worse.

I reached into my bag of tricks and decided to back off and lightheartedly rehearse the passage with a casual "come on guys let's see what we can do" attitude. Need I tell you how that went? Again, I reached into my bag of tricks, this time, so far that I hit floor. After what seemed like a decade of trying, which included moving on and coming back to it, working it slowly, my showing disappointment, working it with its subdivision being played on a snare drum, and everything but my attempting to juggle, I started to feel as though the only thing left, the last resort, was for me to get surly. I began rehearsing with that nasty tone of voice, and after a few moments of it succeeding like the voyage of the *Titanic*, I stopped dead in my tracks, and decided on a different path: they needed a story.

I stopped the group firmly and with no explanation began my saga. "Years ago," I said with a knowing grin, "I was away conducting in a very small, absolutely beautiful town in the middle of nowhere. I mean nowhere. I mean the 'big city' closest to nowhere was still in the middle of nowhere!" After a wonderful festival, I continued, one of the other conductors and I needed to stay over an extra night before we could fly home. After talking with several folks from the community, we decided to take in a movie at the local cinema. In the center of this wonderful town, this beautiful old movie theater from a long-gone era still had a pit for the orchestra.

Worried this little theater wouldn't have refreshments, we decided to grab some candy from a general store next door. Though we had only met a few days before, the other conductor and I made short order of choosing our treat: *Peanut M&M's*. Not a small bag, or a large bag, or even the extra large bag. We bought the jumbo bag; you know, the "no-two-human-beings-should-ever-be-able-to-eat-this-much-candy-in-one-sitting" size bag! Proud of our efforts, we went to the theater and sat down in the very back of the hall. Having no willpower, we decided it was time to break into the candy. I was assigned the easy task of opening the bag. Holding each side of the top of the bag, I pulled in opposing directions. My gentle tug didn't succeed. I pulled a bit more firmly. That too failed. So I tugged with even more force, it turns out with *just enough* force to rip the bag completely open, and I do mean completely. At that moment, every single M&M fell to the very steeply sloped cement floor and began to roll toward the front of the theater. After the initial shock of those sweet gems hitting the floor, and the blood-curdling stare from my "partner-in-candy," I thought I was in the clear as I sat there mortified with embarrassment. I was wrong. The "fun" was still to come.

To my horror, every single piece of the "no-two-human-beings-should-ever-be-able-to-eat-this-much-candy-in-one-sitting" size bag rolled to the front of the hall in a massive race for freedom, then began the downward fall six feet onto the cement floor of the orchestra pit below. No words can describe what that waterfall of M&M's sounded like. Trust me, it was awful. It was like a million little points of sound attacking at random. "Now," I continued, "what could my little story have to do with this rehearsal, you ask? The way you are playing that passage sounds just like my M&M's." After a few moments of laughter, we tried the passage again.

It was perfect. I even repeated it to make sure it wasn't luck; again it was perfect. Why? How? I gave no instructions, I gave no corrective information, I did nothing but make them laugh and get them to envision how bad their original execution of those measures sounded. It wasn't just that the pressure was off; I had tried that to no avail. It wasn't because of the brief respite from re-hearsing it; I tried that too. All I know is within seconds of hearing that dumb story it was beautiful.

That rehearsal reminded me that we should move toward our goal sometimes by running at full speed, sometimes by walking, sometimes by heading straight to it, and sometimes by going a round-about way. But sometimes, the trick may be that however we get there, we should get there laughing. It beats surly most every time. As the Chinese proverb goes, "It is better to laugh at one moment of anger than to regret all the moments to come."

When that evening's rehearsal was over, I stood in the band-room talking with several graduate students as the hall emptied.

As we were chatting, the rehearsal room doors opened and in ran two sophomores from the band: two of my pride and joy. They proceeded to run over and give me two jumbo bags of *Peanut M&M's*, saying, "Here, we ran out and got these to make up for the ones you lost!" I was overwhelmed. It's amazing: just when I am sure I truly appreciate my students and know how incredible they are, they outdo themselves. I didn't know whether to laugh or cry. So after they left, on my way home, I did both.

After eating an entire bag, I kept the wrapper. I use it to this day in the session I present on motivation, discipline and inspiration. It will always remind me of them, of how lucky I am to have had such wonderful students to share my life with, and of the day I chose a better path.

Conducting: "Speak Sparingly and Carry a Meaningful Stick"

M usic lives only when the notes fly off the page and soar into glorious sound. The performer, the conductor, releases them from bondage through his or her feeling for their message, through the power of the imagination, and by means of the physical technique one devotedly acquires. We build the technique *only* to ensure that *our music* can achieve its unforgettable moments, evanescent as they are, before once more returning to its prison of impatient silence. The most profoundly inspiring performances of a lifetime were those where the performer's technique was so superb that we forgot it existed. Music spoke its own language in its own way, uninfluenced by human frailty.

Those remarkable words are the "Credo" from Elizabeth Green's *The Modern Conductor.* In those few sentences, Professor Green offers the essence of all that makes conducting such a special art, all that makes conducting such an illusive art, and all that makes great conducting so very powerful. But how do we reach those heights of human communication? How do we become more passionate, evocative, expressive and communicative, especially if that is not naturally one's personality?

How do we become more creative with our interpretation and conducting of a work? What follows are ideas to open that vista of imagination and communication, to fuel the fire that is a desire to "ensure that *our music* can achieve its unforgettable moments, evanescent as they are, before once more returning to its prison of impatient silence."

Creative Conducting and Interpretation

Does it seem to you that some people are naturally more creative when it comes to interpreting and conducting a score? Do they appear to have an ease or freedom which allows them to be more creative? Do they appear to work with a seeming sense of creative abandon? Is it that they are truly more creative, or is it that they have learned to balance their inner forces to foster creativity? I believe many of us have learned to shy away from trying new ideas, from being creative, out of fear of our inner "judge." Let me explain.

In his book, *A Kick In The Seat Of The Pants*, Roger von Oech describes aspects of how we are creative: "I've concluded that the creative process consists of us adopting four main roles, each of which embodies a different type of thinking." He goes on to describe what he calls the explorer, artist, judge and warrior. Our explorer is open to new ideas, wide-eyed and adventurous. The artist is creative and a bit crazy. The judge is critical and always the naysayer, while the warrior is persistent and determined to work toward any goal.

Each of those dispositions is present within us. When each is balanced by the others, we can flourish as creative individuals. However, when we get stuck or bogged down by any one of them, our creative efforts can be derailed. If our explorer dominates, we will always be looking for places that need creative ideas, never spending enough time refining and working on those ideas. If our artist takes over, we will use every moment coming up with creative, sometimes far too creative solutions that will not be tempered for reality by our judge. Sadly, if our judge becomes boss, as seems so often to be the problem, we pan ideas far too early and often. We say "that won't work" too easily and frequently, often with reasons that are pretty close to "because I said so, *that's* why." When our warrior dictates our thoughts, we spend all our energy trying to make an idea work, even when it should be abandoned or sent back to the artist for reworking.

That's the beauty of this way of thinking. It is not a single linear-sequential approach from one to the next. We move back and forth among the roles to help the process. The artist needs to check with the explorer to see if the idea fits the need. The artist needs to bounce ideas off of the judge to see if they can work. The warrior needs to confirm with the artist all of the vital aspects of an idea. As conductors, we need to develop all four of those roles, constantly moving from one to the others, not allowing any of them—*especially not* our judge—to take over. As Dave Barry quipped: "Never be afraid to try something new. Remember, amateurs built the ark; professionals built the *Titanic*."

Creativity in Interpretation

Commit. The first step in this process—the most important step—is to commit to the music. To truly, unabashedly, spiritually, technically, logically and emotionally commit to the music. Jay Friedman, writing about the late Rafael Kubelik, stated it perfectly: "When he conducted, he was not an interpreter, or the composer, but the score itself. His arms were charged lightning rods through which the score passed." Our interpretation, whether speaking of technical or emotional considerations, comes from our knowing the score cold. Not just knowing enough to travel from measure one to the end, but to realize, savor and be able to point out to our charges all the "sights along the way." In rehearsals, if we are staring at the score, how can we be that kind of guide for others?

We need to connect with each pair of eyes in front of us, spending as little time as possible bobbing up and down—like we are coming up for air while playing an odd game of musical water polo—looking at the score. As an aside, do you know how much the average human head weighs? Have you ever thought about that? It weighs about eight pounds. That's eight pounds of weight we are throwing forward and back as we oscillate from the score to our ensemble. That is as much a strain on the muscles of the neck and back as it is an obstacle to communication with our ensemble. As an even greater aside, have you ever thought about how they figured out how much a human head weighs? That notwithstanding, it all boils down to our knowing the directions for our journey so well we don't need to check the map very often. And we don't just want to know *how* to get to each town on our trip; we want to know everything about each of them.

In the great words of comedian George Carlin, "It's not enough to know which notes to play, you have to know why they need to be played." And that comes only from knowing the score, from committing to the score. We cannot settle for allowing our students, as a result of our abilities and imagination, to play the black and white of the page without bringing it to life with vibrant colors of fluorescent orange and brilliant neon blue. No matter how bogged down we may get with the day-to-day activities of the teaching profession, we need always allow ourselves the time—finding it somehow—to study our scores. We must always find time for our art, working toward finding the beauty of truth held prisoner on the page.

Look for Unity Versus Variety. We all spend so much time working on a balanced, blended, synthesized, corporate, melded sound, that we often don't take advantage of those moments of contrast composers offer us. We must find those buried treasures and bring them to the fore. Granted, much of our music requires a "homogenized" sound, but when it doesn't, when composers balance unity with variety or contrast, we must savor that gift.

At times when my ensembles incorrectly homogenize their playing, I tell them they sound like "milk." I go on to ask them if they drink milk. They usually say "Yes." Then I ask them if milk always tastes the same. They say it does. I tell them milk always tastes the same because producers take millions of gallons of milk from millions of different cows and then blend it all together and homogenize it. In that way milk always tastes the same, rather than one gallon being easily identified as milk from "Bessie the Cow," another from "Daisy the Cow," and yet another from "Susie-May the Cow." I know it's a silly analogy, but it's so very true. There are times our ensemble needs to sound as one, but there are just as many times our students need to relish the contrast each of them may be called upon to provide—and we can help them discover their ever-changing roles.

The Architecture of Details. When studying a composition, we know how important it is to focus on finding the smallest of details. They are certainly the tiny events or ideas that can make a work come to life. However, sometimes it is how *we view* those details that matters most. First we need to view details within the context of the big picture, where the whole work is the "forest" in which "trees" of detail exist. Then we must figure out how the smallest details relate to each other to form the big picture; in other words, how the composition is *the context* in which all details exist, and that the details all *contribute to make* the whole. One without the other yields little. Both together allow for the *architecture* of the work to be clear and profound. A room with the most beautifully designed and trimmed window loses all value if the window is placed so one looks out onto the cement wall of another house.

With music, like architecture, the details must serve the overall design, and vice versa. Try viewing the composition as a blueprint for a home: each detail must serve the room, as each room must serve the design of the house. The flow of each room to the next is as important as the room itself. The overall look of the entire home is no more or less important than whether each room has enough closet space. Where a door is placed is just as vital as how it is framed. The smallest detail of a room's crown molding serves the house just as much as the house's roofline does. Support beams are certainly necessary for structure, but if they are seen, they are an obstacle to flow and beauty.

Great music can easily be viewed in terms of great architecture. Using that image often can be invaluable.

Anything Repeated. *Why* would *you* say the same words twice? Why *would* you say the same words *twice*? Have *you* ever *thought* about that in terms of a musical composition? Have you *ever* thought about that in terms of a *musical* composition? Okay, I'll stop. But I hope the point is clear. Why *would* you say the same words twice? For emphasis? To focus stress on various words within the sentence? To allow the portrayal to carry different emotions? Yes. We need to study anything that is repeated to figure out why it was repeated. Look for differences, even extremely subtle ones. Was it repeated for emphasis, like a refrain? Was it repeated to allow different inflections by stressing different tones, such as when a sentence is repeated with stress on different words: "It was a very *dark* and somber day, a *very* dark and somber day."

Characters in a Play. Relating a musical composition to a play can be very liberating and allow your fertile imagination to take hold. Try thinking of the piece in terms of characters telling a story, like a play. Whether the work is programmatic, and you are following that "script" in your mind, or there is no story behind the piece and you are creating one, think of different sections of the ensemble as characters portraying a story. As with any good play, there will be background information to set the stage, introduction of characters, personalities emerging, a vivid storyline, climaxes, episodes, interludes, reprises and a conclusion.

A Dream. Sometimes I like to think of a composition as if it were a dream. With reality suspended, the only limit to my creativity is my imagination. The story of a play needs to make some sense; however, dreams do not. They can be a bit crazy, illogical and far-fetched. They can allow you to think more like Dr. Seuss than Tolstoy.

A Cartoon. One of my favorite ways to intensify the creativity of the imagination, when it comes to portraying a work, is to think less in terms of a play and more in terms of a cartoon. Why? What's the difference? Both tell a story or portray an image. However, the characters and storyline are far more exaggerated in a cartoon. Think about it: cartoons allow characters to be more like caricatures, with exaggerated emotions, expressions and actions. They are bigger than life, often what we may want a passage in a composition to resemble.

A Sentence. Another way to think of a musical line or phrase is to think of it as you would a sentence, complete with syntax, grammar and punctuation. How easily a sentence changes meaning with different punctuation. The use of one single comma can change the entire thing. An exclamation point, period or question mark can make for markedly different connotations. The rise and fall of inflection, the subtle flexibility of pace, the stress of different words, all allow us to create infinite variety from the same set of words in a sentence, just like those factors allow for the same elements of variety in a set of musical tones.

Talk to Yourself. When trying to become more communicative, asking yourself pointed questions can sometimes be very helpful. Whether it's to help force you to make some interpretive decisions or to illustrate the need for more in-depth study, you can be your own best guide. Try thoughts like:

- What is your favorite phrase or note and why?
- Exactly at what moment is the climax of a section, phrase or movement of the work?
- How does a certain note or phrase make you feel?
- Make up a sentence that describes what you want that certain note or phrase to sound like, what you want it to say.
- What does that phrase or note mean to you?
- What does that phrase or note mean to the composition as a whole?

Projecting the Image of the Work

Once we have committed to the music, thoroughly learned it and made it part of us, we must ensure that we can project the image of the work. Once the magic of the music lives in us, we must make certain that magic lives through us for our ensemble to see and feel. We need to be the physical representation of the musical sounds and emotional context which represent the composer's intent.

I liken this to how great actors and actresses practice their art. They must learn and study a script in solitude: finding every detail of the plot, the setting and their character. Then, after seemingly endless hours of *committing* to the script and their part, they *become* the character. Its portrayal has oozed into every vein and seems to want to come out of every pore of their being. They almost can't help but *be* that character. In that way, if we savor the exploration of a score and the discovery of what it has to reveal, we will become that music; better put, our face, body and hands will have no choice but to embody and emulate that music. We will become the music we seek to portray. Then we can seize and cherish every moment of conducting as an opportunity to create and share wonder, beauty and passion, conducting the music rather than the notes. To serve that end, as much as score study is the given, we must also constantly work to better our technique so as to enable us to physically represent anything our imagination conjures up.

No matter how prepared we are, or how intense our score study has been, it is all for naught if our hands and face are not able to portray what our study has revealed. As well, if our technical ability is limited, our mind will limit our interpretations and revelations of art to those we *can* conduct. That is the embodiment of Abraham Maslow's phrase, "When the only tool you own is a hammer, every problem begins to look like a nail." Much of what we see, interpret and conduct is seen the same way if our conducting technique is weak. If our hands are only able to be hammers—all beats start to look like nails.

Thoughts on the Technique of Conducting

Before delving into the following technical considerations, I would like to spend a moment discussing that word: "technique." Whenever I think of technique, I immediately assume mechanical feats of speed, dexterity and agility, whether it be practice toward playing a passage faster than the speed of light or physical accomplishments that more closely resemble gymnastics than conducting. But I also immediately think of soulless, unemotional, unfeeling, machine-like "successes."

Ask twenty people to define technique, and you will probably get something like that which is stated above. To most, technique is mechanical and physical, as opposed to expressive and artistic. Interestingly, nothing could be farther from the truth.

The word technique actually comes to us from the Greek word *tekhne*, meaning "art." Isn't that amazing? It wasn't the science or the mechanics, it was the art. Technique had one purpose: to serve art. It was the vehicle by which art was made manifest. However, when technique—viewed as sheer physical ability—becomes all that matters, the result is often music devoid of art. Undoubtedly, we must possess the technique needed to accomplish our artistic goals, but we can never lose sight of the fact that the purpose of technique is to serve art; it is art.

A Picture is Worth a Thousand Words. Many of us rely on our words to project the image of our musical intentions. Surely, some things must be explained with words; however, that often becomes a crutch, replacing with lengthy statements that which can be described better by our hands and face. We can never forget that people remember what they see three times longer than what they hear. Though we need both words and hands, we must stay ever vigilant not to allow the former to lessen our need to further develop the latter.

Functional Versus Impressionistic Conducting. In *Teaching Music with Passion*, I went into detail about our need to view conducting as two sides of a single coin. I think of it in terms of what I call *functional conducting*, the technical data and facts of a work, and *impressionistic conducting*, the emotion and expression of a work. I believe one without the other is useless and futile. Instead, we need to think of our impressionistic conducting being layered on top of our functional conducting. Both must work in tandem, their relative importance changing with every beat.

To help clarify the distinction, let me offer this analogy. Let's say you just bought a new home. Knowing that you love the Victorian period, I offer to remodel your living room into a true Victorian parlor. In your absence, I put down a gorgeous hardwood floor, beautiful wood paneling on the walls, fabulous trim, breathtakingly gorgeous Bradbury wallpaper, stunning brass chandeliers and wall sconces, amazing rugs, wall tapestries and artwork. I then bring you into your new room. Would you immediately run to the walls, pounding frantically as you yelled, "Where are the studs?" Of course not. You would coo and awe at the beauty around you. You would marvel at the rich and elegant Victoriana before you. Why on earth would you care about the studs?

Then, after you had a few moments to soak in the splendor, I announce that I bought you a gift. It is a four-hundred pound Victorian mirror, and I want you to hang it before I leave. At that second, what had just become the most important feature of your new room? That's right, the studs. We never notice the studs or beams in a room, we notice the wallpaper. But when we need to hang a heavy object, or the wall starts to crack, or the floor starts to bow, those "technical" aspects become paramount.

When everything is going well in a rehearsal or performance, impressionistic conducting is all that is needed and noticed, for the functional is layered so deeply beneath as to be almost invisible. But when someone is lost and needs a cue, or a passage starts to phase and clarity of pulse is needed to recover, functional conducting becomes all that is needed and wanted. Executed well, the two are seamless and integrated. It is simply a matter of effortlessly adjusting the balance of the two, sensing what is appropriate.

Clarity Versus Inspiration. Of all the balancing acts that are the art and science of conducting, this may be the most difficult. Watching a conductor who is oozing emotion and expression with all his heart can be inspiring. However, if you can't find beat three or the release of a *fermata*, it is all for naught. I firmly feel that "technically correct" conducting, devoid of emotion, is inexcusable. However, conducting that resembles fits of ecstasy, but is devoid of clarity, is useless. We must always walk the tightrope of balance between the two.

Don't Reach—Draw. So many conductors limit, if not defeat, their success in communicating with an ensemble by trying to reach out to them with their gestures. Constantly lurching forward, in an effort to connect with performers, fosters a weak portrayal. Reaching and leaning looks feeble and conveys an almost "begging" quality to your efforts. Without question, occasional leaning or reaching may portray your interpretation, where you want those feelings conveyed; however, too much of it sends the wrong message. Instead of thinking about reaching toward them, think of drawing them in to you. Make your gestures and personality magnetic, using face and hands to focus them on you. Remember, we can't reach out to eighty performers—we can, however, draw them all to us.

Steer Them Versus Drive Them. This may seem like semantics but the difference is enormous. So often conductors try to drive an ensemble, being the fuel, engine and compass for the entire ride. That, simply put, can be draining. One may be able to do that for a while, but not for long. Even more disconcerting is that we then never empower the performers with a sense of responsibility and ownership. They must be the fuel and engine. Sure, we must be the starter, the spark that starts the engine, and occasionally may need to help on those "long hills," but we need to transfer the bulk of that responsibility to them.

Then we can worry about steering the car, offering words of encouragement, pointing out the sights along the way and bringing subtleties to how we travel. Think of it this way: we can't carry one hundred people on our backs, but we can surely show them the right direction. If we are always the motor driving them, they will never learn how to build their own engine.

It's a Matter of Time. Strengthening our ability to communicate our intentions and emulate sound in motion requires that we always remember the effects of reaction time, the gap from the moment we show a gesture to when the sound is heard. We must take that into consideration if our communications are to be useful and timely. Reaction time can actually be thought of in two parts: perception time and response time. Perception time is the time needed for performers to realize and process the communication before them. Response time is the time needed for the performers to act upon that information.

For example, perception time is the time needed for a performer to observe a *subito piano* gesture, recall what it is and decide what is required for it to be executed. Response time is the time it takes that performer to send the signals from the brain to all involved parts of the body, and actually perform what is needed to make that sound. Though it is a huge generalization, with many variables, some estimates have each of those requiring up to three-quarters of a second. That's one and a half seconds from seeing your gesture to having the sound come out of their instrument or voice. One and a half seconds! If that doesn't convince us that the preparation of a gesture, whether with our eyes or hands, is all-important, I don't think anything will.

Learning the Rules. My mom was a wonderful painter. All my life I grew up watching her create beautiful canvasses. Sadly, I got none—and I mean none—of that talent from her. I can hardly draw stick figures that resemble people. I vividly remember coming home from school one day when I was in about second grade, very excited about a decision I had made about my future occupation. Upon arriving home, I told my mom I had decided to become a modern artist. Knowing how skilled I was at drawing, she looked puzzled, but nevertheless chimed in with her always-supportive voice, asking what led to my choice.

I went on to explain that during art class we learned about a modern artist who took cans of paint and threw them at the side of a building, and was paid one hundred thousand dollars for his work. Back then, especially to a seven-year-old, that was a lot of money. As only my mom could have, she very kindly talked about the training one needed to reach that level. I simply said something like, "Training, what training, he was chucking cans of paint on a wall!" Mom then proceeded to explain to me that in art, one needs to learn the rules before one can break them. I immediately told her for that much money I'd learn the rules.

Taking me at my word, she asked me to sit down at the kitchen table. She gave me a sheet of blank paper, and told me to draw a perfect circle—freehand. So, I put pencil to paper and quickly drew what looked more like a defective egg. She then went on to repeat and emphasize her directions, stating that it had to be *truly* round. I tried again with no improvement. After a few tries, I gave up on my new-found-though-short-lived career, saying it was impossible. She then took a sheet of paper and with one beautiful, continuous motion made a perfect circle, even taking a ruler to check its proportions after she finished. It was indeed perfect. With a knowing smile, devoid of any ego, she simply reiterated:

"We need to know the rules before we break them."

Though my drawing skills are no better today, her extraordinary lesson has stayed with me always. In painting, no different than in conducting, we need to know the rules, be able to execute the basics well, before we can break the rules. Clear facts must support feeling. Once our conducting technique conveys precise and effective communication, we can break the rules. Conductors can only be free to be creative if they know from what they are free.

Creativity of Gestures: Becoming More Communicative

If our goal is to serve the music by truly emulating sound in motion, we must constantly strive to be limited only by our judgment and wisdom. We must seek to continually develop our imagination when it comes to interpretation, the creativity of our gestures to portray that interpretation, and our ability to fervently communicate that information. One without the others offers little of substance or usefulness. We each must resolve to conduct the music, the essence of the composition, rather than the notes and symbols on the page. We must be the catalyst for our musicians to breathe life into those black dots on a piece of paper. What follows are a few ideas that may help in our efforts to become more creative and communicative—the key to the treasures of our art and shared musical experiences.

Flow

Cheironomy. The history of conducting is fabulously interesting. Though the modern-day conductor standing on a box with a stick is comparatively new to music, we can trace our roots to times and activities far earlier. Whether we look at divided leadership, the use of a mace, or the motions that came to be known as cheironomy, each undoubtedly brought with it certain virtues and weaknesses. Each had its purpose, though in my mind we lost something extraordinary when we abandoned cheironomy. I have always thought that conducting, thus the music and our musicians, would be better served if we could turn back the hands of time to that remarkable musical communication.

Cheironomy, which many believe the earliest somewhat-codified approach to conducting, became necessary when larger "ensembles" of singers needed to stay together when executing chant. Picture twenty monks in a church—without a conductor—offering a beautiful chant: can't you just envision one of them hollering at the saxes (sorry, force of habit!), I mean at the men farthest to one side, about staying together? The phasing must have been disconcerting to say the least. So the noble art of cheironomy was born out of necessity. Cheironomy, the use of hand gestures to indicate melodic shape, simply and succinctly showed the flow of the line. It was a manner of *representing the music*—truly the music. Absent meter and rhythm as we think of it today, it was incumbent upon the conductor to only portray *the flow*: that is, the manner, mood, contour, dynamics, shape, spirit, articulation, phrasing, ebb and flow, speed, energy, arsis and thesis, and expressive qualities of the music—*not* conduct beats.

From the moment the first conducting mace hit the ground, I believe we have spent so much time worrying about beats and meters that we have somewhat distanced ourselves from all that was so wonderful about cheironomy. Certainly this is an overstatement to some degree, but I believe we should always have those monks and their chant in the back of our minds, finding every opportunity we can to reach back in time and borrow the beauty, and connection to the music, of that approach. How? It may be conducting a homorhythmic line with cheironomy, or adding left hand gestures to foster more refined sounds, or simply demanding from our patterns greater attention to the flow, certainly as much or more than to the beats and meter.

Arsis and Thesis. It may also require many of us to re-examine our thoughts about metric weight and beat patterns, especially when it comes to the meaning and application of the concept of *arsis* and *thesis*. Most of us were trained that each beat of a pattern was either one of thesis or arsis, taught to us as strong or weak, respectively. That leads to patterns with lots of beats and very little connective tissue between them, a plodding sort of movement from beat to beat.

Everything changes, however, when we amend our definition of arsis to that of "lifting" rather than weakness. Beats of arsis lift us to the next thesis, and in so doing provide flow, connection, momentum and energy to the next thesis. Interpreted that way, beats of thesis may have more stress, but beats of arsis are anything but weak.

In an effort to connect to our roots in cheironomy, with its attention to shape and flow, and to better harness the power of the arsis/thesis relationship with its lifting motion between beats, try some of the following.

Moving to Sound. Put on a recording of one of your favorite compositions. Close your eyes and move your hands and arms to the music without any beat patterns. Simply find the essence of the line, the flow, and move to it. Have your body capture and emulate the manner, mood, contour, dynamics, shape, spirit, articulation, phrasing, ebb and flow, speed, energy, arsis and thesis, and expressive qualities of the music—*not* conduct beats. Attend to what the music feels like more than how many beats there are, or what design we use to show them. Then try the same technique, adding subtle motions of the body. Connect with every tone and portray how each should be expressed with your hands, face and body.

Moving to What's in Your Mind. Conduct your favorite score in silence, again using no patterns at all. Try to work as much as possible from memory so the score does not become an obstacle, even if you work through small sections at a time. Move your hands, arms and face to express the flow of the work. Absent patterns, you will be free to attend to the truly musical aspects of the work. Capture the image of every musical event and project it without patterns. Look at how and where gestures fall. Paint a picture, tell a story, do a dance, portray an actor's role—do any and all of them—but do it without the aid or hindrance of beat patterns.

Molding Clay. Put on a recording of a subtle, refined, slow, intense, lyrical work. Then, as you sit and listen, pretend to mold a big ball of clay in your hands. I know this may seem like it warrants the use of mood lighting and a lava lamp, but it is fascinating how well it works. Move your hands, wrists, fingers, thumbs and all of those joints as if shaping the sounds you hear. Never letting go of your imaginary clay, force yourself to move fervently. The quiet power of those gestures, and the facial expressions that almost certainly will come along, seem to almost magically carry over into motions of the arms and body. Then try that activity as you work on passages of a score in silence.

Sing as You Move. While preparing a score, "conduct" a short passage or line of the music without beat patterns, as described above, as you sing it aloud. Have your voice portray how you want it to sound, and then allow your voice to empower your hands and face to match that image. Make your hands *move the sound* rather than move *to* the sound. That may sound like word games, but the difference is that of *causing* sound as opposed to *following* sound.

Better put, make certain you give the impression that the energy in your hands is *making* sound rather than *reacting* to sound.

Then sing it again, this time adding beat patterns to your gestures, though still maintaining as much of "the flow" as possible. Lastly, conduct it "normally" without singing, working to emulate the music and all that your previous work captured.

Finger Paint. Do you remember finger painting when you were young? It was so liberating. Think of it: a teacher basically told you to make a mess using your hands and a bucket of paint. Rules? *What* rules? I believe the only rules were *try not to get it on your neighbor* and *don't drink it.* That was it. Oh, why is youth wasted on the young? What I wouldn't give to do that again. In an odd way we do get that chance every time we conduct. Put a recording on and pretend to finger paint on a wall as you move to the sounds, at first without patterns, then with them. Really.

I know it sounds crazy, but it forces us to examine how we use our canvas (or conducting space), the connectivity of our gestures, the fluidity of our motions, and offers another way to merge our movements with what we hear or want to hear. Then try it again in silence, trying to emulate passages from a score. Now if you are really bold, or have a friend who teaches art at an elementary school, try the real thing! Liberating, fun, creative, truly informative and powerfully evocative: what more could one want?

Go Swimming. One of the most productive ways to develop flow, intensity, elasticity, control of motions and the ability to move sound is to conduct with our arms under water. Stand in water up to the top of your shoulders. Start conducting a passage from memory, at first while singing, then in silence. Try it with and without beat patterns. Feel the resistance the water offers. Note how that resistance engulfs all of you. It is not simply pressure against one surface, it is all around you. Try to move as if you are pulling taffy to those sounds in your head.

Blindfold. I know this is starting to sound a bit weird, but this works. Try conducting with a blindfold on: with and without beat patterns, with a recording and in silence, while singing and not. Why does this work? I have no idea, but I know for some, it liberates them. It allows them to experience a sense of freedom and abandon that nothing else provides. Try it, you will be amazed.

Rubber Bands. Go to an office supply store and ask for large (7 by 1/8 inch, also known as size 117B) rubber bands. Connect two of them by looping them through each other. Put an end loosely over each of your wrists. Then start to conduct. Feel the bands provide an element of resistance with every movement. Don't allow the bands to snap as the intensity releases. Instead, feel as though there is tension on the rubber band at all times, even in moments of repose. Allow the band to be like taffy you are pulling as you move to the sounds you are emulating. Whether you do this with a recording, in silence or as you sing to your conducting, it is a wonderful way to practice your connection to the flow.

Spider Web of Rubber Bands. Taking the usefulness of rubber bands one step further, I build a rubber band spider web for each of my conducting classes. It takes a bit of time, but is worth every minute. The purpose is to make a web of interconnected rubber bands to create resistance in every direction as we conduct. Making it is simple; finding a place to build it is the hard part. I use two wooden flats which resemble sections of a stage shell. Any sturdy structure that offers two opposing faces, approximately five feet apart, is fine. Attach three eyehooks on each side: one just over head, one at mid-chest height, and the other just below the waist. Start by stringing two or three rubber bands together to create a long rubber band that horizontally connects the highest eyehooks, then another strand across the lowest eyehooks.

When finished, you will have two single rubber band loops— at about your starting position—to put your hands through when conducting, the rubber bands going around your wrists like "cuffs." Single rubber bands, or longer lengths made from looping bands together, will then connect the two cuffs to each other; each cuff to all but one eyehook, and each cuff to both of the horizontal strands. You then will have what appears to be a spider web of rubber bands radiating from each cuff, as follows:

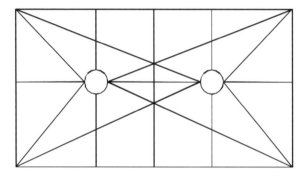

In this way, resistance is created as you move in any direction. No matter how you move, some bands will give way and relax, while others will create resistance. Conducting while bound in this contraption forces you to move in a manner that attends to the intensity of your motions, or intentional lack thereof, at all times. Whether working on the feel of pulling taffy, creating lilt, or portraying a bouncing motion, this device works wonders.

Bubble Wand. This one has to be seen, no, *felt* to be believed. My favorite day of any beginning conducting class is the day we go outside and play with bubble wands. Many years ago, someone gave my children a bubble wand as a gift. The package came with two wands, one with lots of star-shaped holes, the other a single large hoop, as well as a bottle of bubble liquid and a tray. Sitting outside with my kids as they played with this new toy, I noticed the star-shaped one was easy for them, but they got very discouraged with the hoop. I tried it. Instantly, I felt as though I was conducting. The single large hoop required motion that was at once gentle, firm, consistent, intense and replete with resistance. When successful, you could make a bubble which was eight inches in diameter and five feet in length. With practice, you could "turn" the giant bubble, as if creating a loop, and continue making it even longer. It was as difficult as it was productive.

After an hour of playing, and bubble liquid everywhere, I couldn't wait to conduct an ensemble. I felt as though my flow and sense of shaping a phrase had improved immeasurably. Since that time, I recommend bubble wands to every student, for the benefits are as real as the fun doing it.

Slinky. Do you remember that fabulous toy from your youth? It's a wonderful way of developing fine motor skills needed in the fingers, hands, wrists and arms. Simply getting a *Slinky* to move from one palm to the other, spaced an inch apart, requires a great sense of control and dexterity. Then try moving your hands farther apart, making the *Slinky* move over ever-greater expanses, and the difficulty grows significantly. You will find the interrelationship of each part of your musculature deepen with each passing movement.

Hands. One of the great marvels of the human body has to be the hand. With the incredible variety of movements it is capable of and the subtle nuances of expression it can convey, hands can speak volumes if we let them. Often, though, bad habits we develop cause our hands to look odd or stiff. Many of the aforementioned ideas can certainly help the look and communicativeness of our hands, but another trick I like to use is a pair of Velcro mitts. You can find them in toy stores. They are sold as a brightly colored pair of disk-shaped mitts with a *Velcro* tennis ball. They are made for playing catch, but mitts placed on each hand help create amazing-looking hands for the conductor.

The gentle curve of the mitt allows the hand, fingers and thumb to rest on it in a relaxed alignment that is supple and refined, fostering relaxed, elegant hands. In addition, conducting with those mitts on while watching yourself in a mirror easily allows you to identify what part of the hand your ensemble sees. For example, are your palms facing the group, or the back of the hand? Are your hands turned at odd angles? Are they parallel or perpendicular to the ground most of the time? It's not that any one of those answers is always correct or incorrect, but more that the mitts will allow you to easily see what you are doing and when. Then you can be the judge of whether it is what you want to project or not.

A common concern is when fingers seem to look tense and cling to each other. I have found simply holding a pencil between those clinging fingers, close to the knuckle, creates a small space and conditions the fingers to relax. Try that for any of your clinging fingers or thumbs and you will be amazed at how easily the problem disappears.

The Face

Alexei von Jawlensky said, "For me the face is not just a face but the whole universe." I often think of that quote when I look into the eyes of those in my ensembles. I also hope that when they look at me, my face speaks to them. We then could adapt that quote to read: "For our performers, our face is not just a face but the essence of the entire composition." Our face tells the story that is the work we are performing, every mood, every emotion.

Not only do we need to develop those facial expressions, but we need to offer them proactively. By that I mean we should create those facial expressions as we *prepare* our gestures so performers can use them as inspiration to create sounds, as opposed to only using reactive facial expressions created as a *response* to the sound *currently being performed.* Both reactive and proactive expressions are valuable, and both contribute to remarkably expressive communications between ensemble and conductor. For those reluctant to use their faces, or those who wish to further enhance their facial expressions, the following may prove helpful.

The Face and Eyes. Try "conducting," *using only your face and eyes,* first to a recording, then to passages of a score as you sing aloud, then to those passages in silence. Talk about difficult. It is one of the hardest activities I know, but also one of the most beneficial. With no help from beat patterns, hands, arms or body, we must convey as much as possible about the work with only eyes and face. If you want to throw a bit of motion in from the head, that's fine, as long as it is subtle. Do this in front of a mirror, working for powerful, unabashed and overt communication. Remember what our performers see is what we will get. Start by simply singing an expressive phrase of music, then repeating the passage adding facial expressions that truly reinforce your communication.

One of the easiest ways to help ourselves manifest facial expressions is giving a cue. As you conduct a work, or even make one up in your mind, think of how you want to characterize a specific cue. What manner or feeling do you want that entrance to portray? Then practice offering that facial expression as you prepare the gesture and cue in your hands and body. Try this exercise with many cues in succession, making each different in character. In that way, we can develop our ability to almost schizophrenically change our facial expressions when needed.

Conducting a *crescendo* or *decrescendo* also seems to help people portray facial expressions. The intensity of that conducting gesture and the sound it represents help generate facial expressions from those reluctant to do so. Try this exercise: while conducting a four pattern, conduct a two-measure *crescendo* followed by a two-measure *decrescendo*. Start the exercise with your face and hands describing the feeling of sad. Every two measures, change the emotion you are portraying. Use the intensity, power and subtle control of the *crescendo* and *decrescendo* to help evoke those feelings.

Use your imagination and be uninhibited. Emulate the sounds of angry, happy, regal, a sunrise, lightheartedness, contemplation, pouting, exhausted ecstasy, and anything else your mind and soul can create. Make certain your face portrays the energy over every barline. Whether it's building or waning energy, those moments are some of the most fragile and intense in music, and sometimes can be expressed more powerfully by the face than by the hands.

One of my favorite ways to test our ability to communicate from the face is to do a guessing game. Find a partner. The first person writes down ten emotions or expressions she wishes to show using only her face and body language. That person then portrays each one for the other person, who has to guess what is being described. It's like charades using only the face to describe feelings or emotions. It is enjoyable, productive and revealing.

Can the techniques stated above seem artificial and detached from the music? Does it seem that I am advocating theatrics as opposed to truly felt emotions? Yes, but only as a first step in getting people to use their faces. For people who communicate naturally and effortlessly from the face, these exercises are unnecessary. Those people simply attach their facial expressions to the sounds they imagine and the communication is intense and real.

However, for those who find communicating with the face difficult or intimidating, these exercises may provide a way for you to tap into and explore that part of your expressive self. Many people suffer from what I call "facial stage fright." They are simply afraid to use their faces. For them, just making a facial expression, any facial expression, let alone an appropriate one, is a hurdle. After doing these "staged" exercises to express from the face, I think you will find it is easier to *sincerely* apply *appropriate* facial expressions to the music you conduct, facial expressions *the music* will cause you to make.

Specificity

Often it's not the amount of communication but the specificity of that communication we must work toward. At those times, our gestures seem too global. Our conducting communication looks like an army general leading a battle by telling his troops to "Go fight the bad guys," rather than commanding strategic movements and activities for specific purposes. We need to offer conducting gestures that more strategically emulate the sound of a work; for example: attending to a *fortepiano* in the horns while everyone else continues at a *forte* volume, showing a *crescendo* over four beats that only goes from *pianissimo* to *mezzo piano*, or portraying an accent that occurs only in the trombones while all else play *legato*.

Without question, sometimes our gestures must be global in their communication; however, just as often our conducting needs to be extremely specific, targeted and detailed. At those times, our gestures should work like tiny laser beams, directing specific information to a very precise target.

Goal Orientation

Whether it's showing the peak of a phrase, the zenith of a passage or section, the climax of a movement or entire work, or carrying a phrase over a barline from measure to measure, we must never lose sight of the importance of communicating musical goals. We may think of it as flow, contour, shape, structural goals, intensity points or other terms, but they all boil down to our knowing where we are, where we're going, and how. Simply put, we must convey the focus, intensity and movement of our journey in our conducting at all times. Goal orientation must be understood *and communicated* so every note moves toward or away from a small goal and layer after layer of larger goals. Wandering around in the woods can be fun for a while; however, after we realize we don't know where we are going, our sense of security, let alone our purpose, is lost.

Left or Right

I believe much of our ability to communicate clearly and strategically comes from our developing independence of hands, as well as our ability to conduct with only one hand, or both hands in mirror image. Each has its purpose, each can be productive and each can facilitate certain communications more efficiently and effectively.

For subtle passages of almost crystalline delicacy, or solo passages with gentle accompaniment, conducting with only the right hand is extraordinarily effective. However, for passages of more global communication, especially those of lush sustain, powerful intensity or dramatic brawn, mirrored conducting may have greater impact. Let us look at a four pattern to illustrate my point. Though the lift of beat four, and weight or stress of beat one, can be communicated with mirrored conducting as well as conducting with only the right hand, the relaxation of beat two and tension of beat three undoubtedly can be better communicated with mirrored conducting.

When conducting in a mirrored fashion, the contraction of both hands moving inward toward each other shows the relaxation on beat two so vividly. Also, both hands moving away from each other in a gesture of opposition communicate the intensity of beat three clearly and powerfully. Can the characteristics of beats two and three be described with only one hand in motion? Yes, but at times when two mirrored hands can be used, the portrayal will be all the stronger with the ability two hands have to move toward and away from each other.

Though mirrored conducting or conducting with only the right hand can be best for specific passages, more often than not the conducting enabled by true independence of hands provides the most effective communication and the greatest ability to emulate sound in motion. I like to think of the purpose and function of conducting hands like some scientists think of brain function. Though the notion of handedness and brain function is not universally agreed on, it is nonetheless an interesting way to describe the specific function of conducting with independence of hands.

Brain function theory states that the left side of our brain is wired to the right side of our body and vice versa. Though most of us have a side of the brain that is dominant, we use both, just like we use both hands in conducting. We may be more inclined, comfortable and able with one, but both are necessary to some degree. Our left brain dwells on logic, details, facts, rules, order, patterns, data and all that is practical, while our right brain focuses on feelings, context, imagination, fantasy, impetuousness and emotions.

Though both hands can and do portray both left-brain and right-brain characteristics of the music, often an easy way to begin conducting with more independence of hands is to think of our hands like those sides of the brain, having the right hand focus more on conveying the facts and data, such as meter, tempo, and dynamics, while the left hand describes those more subjective details of mood and expression through cues, contour, phrasing, subtle contrasts, or any portrayals that may be in opposition to what the right hand is describing. Eventually, with practice, objective and subjective gestures will flow freely from both hands, blending the use of the hands into one highly communicative canvas.

Choreography

"I want this phrase to sound completely spontaneous. However as the result of meticulous planning." Those words of George Szell, though intended for performers, describe what to me is great conducting. Watching a genuinely remarkable conductor, I am taken with the specificity of the gestures, as well as how refined, extraordinarily communicative, incredibly fluid and effortless they appear. But I am equally taken with how the gestures flow from one to the next like the music they emulate.

Some believe if we know the music well enough, that will happen. To me, that's like saying if a dancer knows the music, the movements and the threading of them together into a synthesized whole will just happen. Certainly, dance movements that are highly skilled and choreographed are worthless if they do not reflect the music itself. They would be technique without art, movements without soul. However, great conducting, like great dance, must be made to look and feel as effortless as it does "spontaneous," both as a "result of meticulous planning" and practice.

Like a dancer practices the choreography of movements, we must choreograph every movement as well as plan and practice how to get to and from each gesture so the final product seems seamless and artistic. Does this require enormous attention to detail? Yes. Will much of that work be specifically observable? No. But let us always remember that the reality of greatness is often found in the *sum* of many tiny, virtually insignificant details.

Once we arrive at gestures that emulate our interpretation of the score—conducting with either both hands mirrored, one hand alone, or with independent gestures in each hand—we can practice the motions of each hand separately, then together, working out the specific movements of each gesture. Equally important, however, is practicing how each hand moves from gesture to gesture, musical event to musical event, and place to place on our conducting canvas. We must especially plan when and how we will disengage our left hand from the pattern before attempting an independent gesture, so as to look smooth and graceful, as well as how we will reengage that hand into the pattern, if so desired. How will our left hand get from one place for one gesture to another place for another gesture, each place descriptive of a desired sound? How will we get to and from gestures that move along our canvas in an effort to describe a specific sound?

That is, how do we move from cueing a light finger cymbal strike off to the left side of our canvas, above our head, to showing a mournful bass drone low and forward on our frame, to portraying a slow downward *glissando* for the trombones we emulate by moving diagonally from high and to our right to low and to our left on the canvas?

Inherent in that choreography must be attention to portraying a sense of *follow-through* for all gestures of the left hand, so the end and aftermath of the gesture continues to emulate the intensity or lack of intensity desired. The follow-through of the left hand, how it moves *after* a cue, may be more important than the cue itself in describing that sound. Does that hand follow through from the gesture in a manner which carries forward the feeling of the musical event, or is it so terse and awkward as to resemble more the popping of a soufflé? Does a *crescendo* gesture end with the continued flow of that power in sound and style, or does it look like we simply *abandoned it* for the next gesture? Does the left hand move away from a gesture as if floating off in the distance, emulating the resonance of a bell strike, or does it appear more to be the "thud" of hitting concrete?

Though the above thoughts may seem artistically mechanical, they are offered as tools to begin developing the ability to communicate more specifically and effectively. Eventually this becomes second nature. However, for those looking for a place to start on the road to more effective conducting, these ideas may help spark creativity and give you a sense of empowerment. Quite simply, I think of highly developed conducting skill as the very embodiment of the following words, paraphrased from the music theorist Hugo Norden: Simplicities are made up of infinite complexities and complexities are made up of infinite simplicities. An infinite number of simple gestures, motions and choreography make for conducting that conveys complex communication. However, if done well, one never sees the complexity and is only taken with the simplicity and directness of its message. As Goethe so eloquently put it, "Everything is simpler than you think, and at the same time, more complex than you imagine."

The Process of Subtraction

Often, in an effort to attend to a large *number* of musical details in a work or to project greater *magnitude* to what is already a busy fabric of powerful conducting gestures, we think of adding more and more. In so doing, we constantly increase the quantity and/or size of our gestures. That practice can be exciting and offer a feeling of powerful conducting, but it also can be debilitating, lead to overconducting, and by its very nature become virtually unreadable to performers. So much information is being shown, in such comparatively enormous proportions, in such a short time span, as to make it impossible to decipher. At a certain point, adding gestures in an effort to evangelically emulate more attributes of a work—especially at a fast tempo—becomes unreadable.

The solution, in part, can be found in the words of the renowned architect Ludwig Mies van der Rohe when he stated, "Less is more." So as not to overconduct, or conduct more than can be absorbed, sometimes we need to reduce, or *subtract*, from view or emphasis what isn't needed rather than increase what is to be featured. By contrast then, certain gestures will be perceived as being emphasized, not by their being bigger, but by all else being smaller. Someone far smarter than I will have to determine if William James was right when he said, "The art of becoming wise is the art of knowing what to overlook." But certainly knowing what to ignore or downplay can be key to more effective and communicative conducting.

Assessing Our Conducting

WHO'S RIGHT?

Conducting, possibly more than anything else in music, is incredibly subjective. There are as many different approaches as there are conductors, each fervent in their beliefs. Truthfully, that's what makes the art of conducting so exciting and varied. That is also what makes it somewhat difficult to assess. One need only review all the conducting method books available, let alone watch the many gifted conductors of our day, to discover firmly held ideas that can be quite disparate. With those vast differences, how does one assess the quality of one's conducting?

Ultimately, we must be the final judge of what works for us and what doesn't. Even more, our student performers will help us to understand what works and what doesn't. Their performance at any given time gives us immediate feedback about the effectiveness of our conducting. As I have said before, they are the perfect mirror. Whether it is due to a lack of clarity, correctness, appropriateness or specificity, if our conducting fails to achieve the desired result, we have our assessment.

WHAT'S WRONG?

So often, it's easy to see we have a problem with our conducting; knowing what's wrong and how to improve it is what's difficult. It's always easier to find fault with something than to know what to do to make it better. By way of example, if we taste a soup and it is far too salty, it's easy to assess the flaw. However, simply reducing the salt would not necessarily make for a wonderful recipe. The stellar chef knows how to use each different ingredient in a way that will make a soup in which the flavors meld so well that they create perfection— just like we need to do with the many facets of our conducting.

Whether we are assessing our conducting to correct severe problems, to eradicate bad habits that slowly have crept in over time, or to make our already extremely effective conducting even better, we all need regular doses of constructive criticism. Receiving that from expert teachers is wonderful and extraordinarily valuable; however, eventually we all need to become our harshest and most demanding critic. As Walter Anderson observed, "Our lives improve only when we take chances—and the first and most difficult risk we can take is to be honest with ourselves." But how?

SEEING IS BELIEVING

Videotaping our conducting in rehearsals, on a regular basis, is a wonderful tool most people find very revealing. With the camera behind our ensemble, aimed at *our* faces, we see what our students see. Critical evaluation of our gestures will help identify problems, areas of concern which need further assessment, and aspects that are good but could be made even better. Helpful as that can be, going one step further can be even more enlightening.

DOING IS BELIEVING EVEN MORE

At one of those videotaped rehearsals, conduct a complete run-through of a piece. Later, when you have a bit of free time, put a chair and music stand in front of a television monitor set up to play back that videotape, just like you would if you were an ensemble member and that television were your conductor. Now, using the same music the students use, with the sound of the television turned off, sing your voice part or play your instrument to the tape, as if you were one of your own students—following *you*. How's that for "A picture is worth a thousand words?" What do you see? Whatever it is, that's what your students see.

Start with the functional information. Could you find the tempo from the initial preparatory gesture? How easily could you follow the beat patterns? Did those patterns reflect the arsis and thesis of the meter? Was the pulse steady? Did each rebound prepare the next beat? Were all of the gestures prepared enough, and given with enough reaction time to make them executable? Was there a lot of over-conducting? Did the style of the motion impart a sense of the articulation, flow and contour of the line? Were the dynamics clear? Were cues and releases appropriately conveyed? Were the eyes of the conductor on the score or on the ensemble?

Then move on to matters of impressionistic conducting. Did you see intensity, drama, mood, style, emotion and expression? Did you see them from the hands as well as from the face? Did what you see make you want to return those feelings through your performance? Did the portrayal make you want to give of yourself—your inner self? Did the music seem to live through the motions you watched? Did they make you want to play or sing from the heart? Were you moved or were you bored? Could you connect with that person on the television screen? Even more importantly, did you *want* to connect with that person?

In short, how often did you have to ask, "I wonder what that gesture meant?" Sometimes what we see is startling enough that we find ourselves more pointedly asking, "The heck with what that gesture meant, *who* is *that person?*"

WHAT THEY *DON'T SEE* IS WHAT WE WANT

Another way we can challenge our ability to communicate as conductors is to hand out a piece to our ensemble from which we have carefully removed every marking except the notes on the staff, key and meter signatures, barlines and rehearsal numbers. That's right, after getting permission from the copyright holder, sit down with a big bottle of *Wite-Out* and remove every descriptive word, fermata, dynamic marking, articulation, phrase mark, speed indication—everything but the bare bones. With our musicians now armed with nothing but the notes and rhythms, it is completely up to us to convey every detail and nuance of the "real" music—the essence of what is beyond the notes.

It does take a lot of time and effort, but it is the single most challenging, somewhat frightening, yet amazingly rewarding activity I know for any conductor. At that instant we must *become* the music. We must *portray* the music. We must truly *emulate* the music. The music must live in us and through us. Try it; I'm sure you will be glad you did.

Conclusion

Have you ever stood there conducting your ensemble, watching your students' faces as they perform, listening to the sounds you are helping them create, feeling the emotions you are sharing with them and thought to yourself, "Amazing, utterly amazing!" That you can do so much with nothing but your hands, mouth, face, mind and heart, never ceases to amaze me. No tools, no machines, no supercomputers, no electricity, just gestures, motions and expressions that say so much with so little.

As much as we study the art and science of conducting, even though we can objectively explain what is going on, I really don't think anyone can really describe it completely. There is magic at its core. There are moments that can only be described as nothing short of telepathy. How can a single motion connect human beings as one? How can a facial expression tell an entire story? How does a glance from one person's eyes speak directly to another person's soul? I don't know, but I marvel at it every time I stand before an ensemble, humbled by the magic and that which it provides.

Why is conducting so important to our teaching and the education of our students? I guess it all comes down to one simple thought by E. H. Gombrich: "Anyone who can handle a needle convincingly can make us see a thread which is not there." That thread, to me, is passion, communication, expression, soul and feelings. It is the thread that makes all the difference in the world.

Each of us must continuously strive to improve our ability to communicate through conducting so as to make real the remarkably profound words of Goethe: "Things which matter most must never be at the mercy of things which matter least." Our conducting, those physical gestures "which matter least," can never stand in the way of our ability to help young people communicate "that which matters most": the essence and power of music.

A Conductor's
Warm-Up

"Dear Peter," the letter began, "I am at home having recently returned from the hospital. I am in incredible pain, and thought of you." Now picture how you would feel if you received that note. "I just had rotator cuff surgery," he went on to write, "and it really hurts. What's worse is that I will have to return to the hospital in a few months to have the other arm done. I thought of you because I am sure that the cause was my conducting. Twenty years of abuse and my arms just gave out. Having seen so many of your workshops on conducting, I wondered why you haven't done one on how to prevent destroying your career! I just wish someone would have alerted me to how damaging my conducting was."

I am sad to say that this is but one of a great number of letters, emails and phone calls I have received with basically the same story. Another that stands out in my mind was the day a gentleman I have known casually for years walked over to me as I was standing in front of a booth at a convention; he began speaking to me in a frantic manner. He told me that after twenty years of conducting he was in great pain and he feared, from conversations with his physician, his career may be in jeopardy. He went on to ask what I did to prevent that kind of damage. Wanting to help, I said I would be glad to chat with him about it later. He immediately said, "No, let's do it right now." I told him I needed to stay at the booth for a while, whereupon he proceeded to take off his sport coat, implying there was no time like the present. I showed him a few exercises, and suggested he see a professional to find other exercises that would target his specific condition. I have to tell you that I felt like a complete idiot standing there in the exhibition hall of a convention doing stretching exercises more fitting to a gymnasium.

The purpose for my telling these stories is that these kinds of problems happen more often than you could imagine. When they do, it is frightening, debilitating, painful and frustrating. Picture it: something you love doing that is central to your expressing your art is causing you discomfort and may have to be stopped permanently. If it hasn't happened to you, consider yourself lucky and take steps to prevent it from ever happening. Now you may be saying to yourself, "I am in great shape and I work out twelve hours a day; this can't happen to me!" Or, "I am only twenty-three years old; that is only something that happens to older folks." Wrong! I know many young conductors whose ailments began very early in their teaching careers, and many very athletic people whose exercise regimens, though wonderful for some aspects of life, do nothing to aid these specific problems.

Why do we have these problems? Often the source is frustration with our conducting, which leads to overconducting and a lack of awareness of these potential occupational problems. It is unfortunate that some conducting classes do not teach or stress the importance of a daily warm-up routine for conductors. Then right out of college, conductors can get away with using (or abusing) their bodies in a manner that may eventually cause damage because youth provides an element of resilience. Unfortunately, that damage may not appear for years. Let's face it, when we were in undergraduate school we thought we were indestructible. Maybe to some degree that was true, but those bad habits learned early on may wear on the body, appearing as problems later in life.

We need to protect ourselves from damage, especially from wear and tear caused by our conducting. Athletes are taught how *not* to damage themselves when doing certain physical activities. But conductors rarely are. Physical education teachers always teach cross-country runners how to stretch before a race. Conductors too must warm-up, stretch and align themselves before conducting for hours on end.

A first step is awareness. We need to "listen" to our bodies. Pain or discomfort in any way, shape or form is bad. Nothing we do as conductors should cause any feeling of soreness, tenderness, grinding, popping or snapping of tendons, joints or muscles. The ability to conduct for long periods of time without fatigue or discomfort comes from using the body in a natural, comfortable and aligned way so as to prevent unnecessary strain or damaging movements. Of course, after ten hours of rehearsing, one is dead tired. The brain, voice, ears, patience and feet may be shot, but if we conduct correctly, with the proper warm-up and stretching, damage doesn't enter the realm of possibility.

We each need to assess our conducting with a critical eye to movements damaging to the body, finding correct motions to replace them. In addition, I advocate a few minutes of constructive warm-up exercises every morning, and before rehearsals. Before you think I am suggesting getting out the old exercise clothing, I really mean a few minutes. My morning routine takes less than three minutes and then I follow it up with a minute or so before the start of every rehearsal. That may not seem like much, but I think those few minutes help settle my mind as well as my body and may prevent physical problems down the pike. I truly believe a few minutes every day could help some people extend their careers. With that at stake, are a few minutes too many?

We each must develop a warm-up routine that helps us. Depending on your preferences, that could come from a physician, sports trainer, physical therapist, chiropractor or Alexander Technique practitioner. We each need to see a professional in the field to learn how to help ourselves. And though I don't want to sound like one of those exercise equipment television commercials, I always counsel people to see a physician before they attempt any such routine.

My routine starts by simply standing up, grounding my body correctly, and gently swinging my arms forward and backward. That calming activity allows me to make certain my body is relaxed and aligned correctly. Then I do a series of stretches by gently pulling one arm across my stomach, from one side to the other, parallel to the floor, using my free hand to smoothly and lightly pull that arm from the elbow. I go very slowly until I feel a subtle stretching feeling. Then I hold my arm there for a few seconds before even more slowly allowing it to return back to the starting point. I do this for each arm twice.

Next I go to the corner of a room. Facing the corner, I take a small step or two backwards. I put both of my hands flat against the wall, just in front of my shoulders, and slowly use my arms to do a vertical "push up" toward the corner of the wall. I usually do that twice, each time taking ten seconds to move forward, ten seconds holding in the corner, then ten seconds to move back away from the wall.

Having said this, please do not try these without talking to a professional first. Just because that routine helps me does not mean it will help you. For that matter, it may cause you harm. Only a healthcare provider will know. Please do not put this off. See someone you think can help you come up with a warm-up and then religiously do it every day!

It may be like the old joke about the man who invents a pill that when taken regularly prevents one from seeing pink elephants: you may never know if it works. But I think the risk of not doing something is just too great. Don't make a physician tell you that you will have to stop conducting.

I teach my students how to warm-up in conducting classes, but more significantly, they see me do it for a minute or so just before rehearsals. In that way, I hope to reinforce its importance by letting them know I don't just say it, I do it. My hope is simply to prevent them from ever having to write a letter like the one at the beginning of this chapter. ▒

INDEPENDENCE OF
HANDS

Freedom. A remarkable word. And when it comes to conducting, that's what it's all about. Freedom to use our arms and hands in any way we wish to convey our interpretation of the music. So the only constraint we have is the limit of our imagination, not our physical ability to move in a way which could bring that imagination to life. "A musician's fingers are the ultimate dancers," Bruce Adolph wrote, "they call the tune and dance it into existence." And the ultimate expression of that wonderful sentiment is conducting, where we truly do call the tune, and must "dance" it into existence in the minds, hearts and souls of our students.

But often I hear from people that they lack confidence in their ability to portray the music as they wish, because they lack confidence in their physical ability to conduct the gestures they wish to use. They simply feel unable or insecure when it comes to the physical aspects of conducting. Whether one is working toward better portraying elegant cues, unobtrusive page turns, fluid beat motion, more vivid dynamic contrasts, or is wishing to have the ability to show two different communications at the same time, paramount in gaining those skills is developing true independence of hands. By that I mean the ability to have each of our arms and hands move with complete independence and resolve. That technical skill will allow us the freedom to conduct anything we can imagine. Anything.

One could argue this training is purely technical in nature, conducting calisthenics, if you will. And that's true, but as Bruce Adolph went on to write, "Technique for a musician is the flower which blooms in order to celebrate the fruit; it is reality, which is the only path to mystery." That technique allows us to portray our interpretation with the clarity of our intentions, to ultimately reveal the essence of a work. What we develop as purely physical, technical skill manifests itself in our ability to emulate sound in motion, to physically represent the music, to more effectively help those we conduct envision how best to play in an effort to capture the "truth" of those fuzzy little black dots on a sheet of white paper.

What follows is a series of exercises to develop independence of hands. Over the years, I have used these exercises to take students from "square one" to relative freedom of expression. The exercises are sequential in nature, and should be done step by step. Though it may seem that certain exercises are redundant, each builds upon the previous step and develops some dimension of this ability, and should not be skipped. Work to become relatively confident with an exercise before moving on to the next. In order to protect your joints and musculature, please remember to "warm-up" by stretching appropriately. Make every effort to move smoothly, freely and very slowly, the slower the better. In fact, the slower and smoother the motion, the more it fosters the independence we seek.

Also, make certain to keep good posture and stance, with head, neck and body orientation/alignment conducive to freedom of motion. Keep all movements in front of you in a comfortable two-dimensional "frame" of motion, staying no higher than the top of your head, *no lower than your waist* and only modestly wide. Never allow your arms, especially elbows, to rear back along the sides of your torso. Keep your palms basically facing the floor, allowing them to follow the same angle as your lower arms. Again, it's all about looking, feeling and moving freely, smoothly and effortlessly. It is without question the quality of the motion, not the quantity, that matters.

Exercise 1: "Rub and Pat." Though this may cause flashbacks to days in kindergarten, and may seem sophomoric to say the least, it is a wonderful first step. Simply have one hand move up and down over your head as if patting it, while the other hand makes circular motions just in front of your stomach as if rubbing it. Make certain that neither hand actually touches the head or tummy, and that the motions are strictly a vertical straight line or truly round circle, respectively. I caution this only because I have seen many a person with circular tapping and vertical rubbing, or some kind of mutant hybrid in both hands, who thinks, because his mind's eye is lying to him, he is letter perfect. To prevent this, occasionally practice each of these exercises in front of a mirror so you can *see the truth*. However, don't always practice them that way since you will want to wean yourself from your actual eyes to your mind's eye.

The next step is to randomly switch the role of each hand so the one that was rubbing the tummy becomes the one patting the head, and vice versa. Continue to switch back and forth at will, working for those changes to be effortless and immediate. Guard against rubbing motions that start as pseudo-patting or patting that starts as pseudo-rubbing, as if the hands are *gradually* changing roles. Make the switching, as well as all the movements, appear and feel casual rather than mechanical, not allowing the first motions after the switch to start with an accentuated jolt of coordinated motion. The goal is to change smoothly, instantly and completely.

In addition, we want to work toward freeing our minds as we do these exercises, not using every ounce of concentration to accomplish the task. To that end, after successfully doing this exercise, and all subsequent exercises, go back and repeat the task while doing something that occupies your mind. Some of my favorites are carrying on a conversation with someone, doing math problems in your head, reciting the alphabet backwards, or reading the closed caption text on a television set with the sound turned off. It doesn't really matter what the activity is that challenges our concentration, as long as it does.

Exercise 2: "Vertical/Vertical (Random)." Begin with both hands positioned in front of you as if you were to conduct a piece at a moderate volume, or what I refer to as the *position of rest*. Raise both hands up to about the height of the top of your head, then lower them back to your starting position. Ensure that the motions are truly vertical and not bowed at all. The flexibility provided by the use of each joint of the arm allows for motion that is as accurate as it is elegant and fluid. Make certain never to stop the motion of the hands at anytime.

Once both hands are moving correctly, allow each hand to move independently with random, uncoordinated up and down motions. Remember, the slower and smoother, the better. Moving at different and varying speeds, the two hands should seem totally unrelated, save for being connected to the same body.

In addition to checking the accuracy of your movements with a mirror, for this exercise and all of the exercises that follow, try doing them standing in front of a wall. Facing the wall, allow your outstretched finger tips to gently "draw" the design on the wall. Making certain your finger tips always stay in contact with the wall ensures all the parts of your arm are working in concert, the design is accurate and the image is truly a two-dimensional portrayal on your conducting canvas. Another way to check for these attributes is to occasionally practice an exercise while standing in front of a chalkboard, chalk in hand, actually drawing the design on the board.

Exercise 3: "Vertical/Vertical (Wiggle Fingers)." Repeat the previous exercise having all the fingers in one hand wiggle as they ascend or descend. Randomly pass this wiggling from hand to hand, never allowing both to wiggle at the same time.

Exercise 4: "Vertical/Vertical (Specific Wiggling)." Repeat the exercise above having the left hand fingers wiggle only as they ascend, and the right hand fingers wiggle only as they descend.

Exercise 5: "Vertical/Vertical (Flipping Palms)." Repeat Exercise 2 having one hand flip over as it moves, so the palm is facing upward, while the other hand stays palm facing downward. After a few moments, switch it back. Randomly pass this flipping palm motion between hands. Never flip both hands at the same time, and make certain the vertical motion stays fluid with no jolts or stops.

Exercise 6: "Horizontal/Horizontal (Random)." This is the same as Exercise 2 having the motion in both hands be horizontal, side to side, rather than vertical. Again, use all the parts of the arm to ensure the motion is two-dimensional and in front of your body. Guard against your elbows rearing back by checking your accuracy on a wall or chalkboard.

Exercise 7: "Horizontal/Horizontal (Wiggle Fingers)." Horizontal motion in both hands, with the addition of wiggling fingers as described in Exercise 3.

Exercise 8: "Horizontal/Horizontal (Flipping Palms)." Horizontal motion in both hands, with the addition of flipping palms as described in Exercise 5.

Exercise 9: "Vertical/Horizontal." Move vertically with one hand while moving horizontally with the other. At random intervals, have both hands simultaneously switch between vertical and horizontal motions. Add the wiggling of fingers or the flipping of palms at will.

Exercise 10: "Diagonal/Horizontal." Repeat the exercise above, replacing the vertical motion with a diagonal motion that moves upward and to the side of your body.

Exercise 11: "Circle/Circle (Same Image)." Starting from your position of rest, make large circular motions with both hands moving in a counterclockwise fashion, thus creating the *same* image. Moving at the same speed, both hands should complete each rotation at the same moment. However, for this and all subsequent exercises that call for hands to move "in time," please guard against having them look or feel the least bit mechanical in nature. Once comfortable with this exercise, randomly reverse the direction of both hands simultaneously.

Exercise 12: "Circle/Circle (Mirror Image)." Repeat the exercise above, having the hands move in mirror image of each other, one hand moving clockwise while the other moves counterclockwise.

Exercise 13: "Corkscrew/Corkscrew (Same Image)." This exercise is the same as Exercise 11, with the circles gradually expanding in size from very tiny to quite large in diameter, then back to their starting size. For all exercises involving a corkscrew motion, it is essential to keep the time it takes for a revolution constant, irrespective of the size of the loop. Larger loops will move much faster than smaller loops, but both will complete each revolution at the same time. Again, randomly reverse the direction of both hands simultaneously.

Exercise 14: "Corkscrew/Corkscrew (Mirror Image)." Repeat the previous exercise with hands moving in mirror image of each other as they create the corkscrew motion.

Exercise 15: "Small Circle/Corkscrew (Same Image)." With both hands moving counterclockwise, one hand makes small circles that stay constant in size, as the other hand executes the corkscrew motion. Again, make certain the rotation in each hand ends at the same moment. Randomly reverse the direction of both hands simultaneously.

Exercise 16: "Small Circle/Corkscrew (Mirror Image)." Repeat the previous exercise with hands moving in mirror image of each other.

Exercise 17: "Large Circle/Corkscrew (Same Image)." Repeat Exercise 15, replacing the small circle with a very large circle that stays constant in size. The corkscrew, however, still begins very small before gradually expanding.

Exercise 18: "Large Circle/Corkscrew (Mirror Image)." Repeat the previous exercise with hands moving in mirror image of each other.

Exercise 19: "Small Circle/Large Circle (Same Image)." With both hands moving counterclockwise, have one hand create a very small circle while the other hand makes a very large circle. Be certain both hands maintain the size of their respective circles. Practice this with both hands moving at the same and then at different rates of speed. As well, randomly reverse the direction of both hands simultaneously.

Exercise 20: "Small Circle/Large Circle (Mirror Image)." Repeat the previous exercise with hands moving in mirror image of each other.

Exercise 21: "Corkscrew Bigger/Corkscrew Smaller (Same Image)." Start Exercise 19, having the small circle gradually increase in size using the corkscrew motion, while the large circle gradually gets smaller using the corkscrew motion. Make certain both hands move counterclockwise and finish each rotation at the same time, irrespective of the size of the circles they are creating.

Exercise 22: "Corkscrew Bigger/Corkscrew Smaller (Mirror Image)." Repeat the previous exercise with hands moving in mirror image of each other.

Exercise 23: "Circle/Circle (Alternating Directions)." From your position of rest, have both hands make moderately large circles in a counterclockwise fashion, moving at a constant rate of speed. Try to create a lilting, buoyant, lifting motion as you make your circles. Make four complete revolutions. Then abruptly yet elegantly reverse the direction of your right hand so it is moving clockwise. After four revolutions, reverse the direction of your left hand so it too is moving clockwise. After four revolutions, reverse the direction of your right hand so it is moving counterclockwise. After four more revolutions, reverse the direction of the left hand to move counterclockwise. At this point, you will be back to where you started. Try doing this exercise using any number of revolutions between direction changes.

Exercise 24: "Figure Eights (Same Image)." Start with your hands at a height just over your head, about the width of your position of rest. From that point, begin to move both hands at a constant rate of speed counterclockwise, making the shape of an eight that is the same image in each hand. Use the mirror, wall and chalkboard to make sure your mind's eye is telling you the truth about your design.

Exercise 25: "Figure Eights (Mirror Image)." Start in the same position as the exercise above having your right hand begin by moving counterclockwise as your left hand begins by moving clockwise, thus creating figure eights which are the mirror image of each other.

Exercise 26: "Figure Eights (Opposite Direction/Mirror Image." Begin with your left hand up where it was for the previous exercise and the right hand down at its position of rest. The left hand will start moving clockwise to create a figure eight that will initially move in a downward direction, while the right hand will begin by moving clockwise to create a figure eight that will initially move in an upward direction. In that way, you will create mirror-image figure eights that will be moving in opposite vertical directions.

Exercise 27: "Square/Square (Same Image)." Starting with both hands up in the air as you did for the first figure-eight exercise, have both hands move horizontally to the left, then straight down, then horizontally to the right, and finally straight up to form two squares of the same image. Have both hands move at a constant, steady rate of speed.

Exercise 28: "Square/Square (Mirror Image)." Repeat the exercise above, initially moving the left hand horizontally to the right to create two squares of mirror image.

Exercise 29: "Square/Square (Alternating Images)." This exercise is more difficult to describe than it is to do. Begin with both hands up in the air. From that starting point, do one complete cycle of the "Square/Square (Same Image)," stopping right where you began. Then, from that point, do one complete cycle of "Square/Square (Mirror Image)," again ending up just where you started. Continue to alternate between those two images.

Exercise 30: "Triangle/Triangle (Same Image)." From a starting position up in the air, move both hands diagonally down and to the left, then horizontally to the right, and finally diagonally up and to the left to create two, same-image equilateral triangles that look like pyramids, their points at the top and bases on the bottom.

Exercise 31: "Triangle/Triangle (Mirror Image)." Repeat the exercise above, initially moving the left hand diagonally down and to the right to create two triangles of mirror image.

Exercise 32: "Triangle/Triangle (Alternating Directions)." Start by doing one complete cycle of Exercise 30, "Triangle/Triangle (Same Image)," ending where you started. From that point do one complete cycle of Exercise 31, "Triangle/Triangle (Mirror Image)." Continue to alternate seamlessly between those two images. Done correctly, the triangles created in both images will be the same size and shape.

Exercise 33: "Circle/Horizontal." From your position of rest, have one hand create a circle as the other moves horizontally side to side. No feeling of pulse or coordinated movement should be felt between the hands. The two designs should look totally out of sync with each other. At random intervals, have your hands switch roles. The following exercises should be done in the same manner, creating the designs or shapes indicated. Do not forget to have your hands switch roles at random intervals.

Exercise 34: "Corkscrew/Horizontal."

Exercise 35: "Figure Eight/Horizontal."

Exercise 36: "Triangle/Horizontal."

Exercise 37: "Square/Horizontal."

Exercise 38: "Circle/Vertical."

Exercise 39: "Corkscrew/Vertical."

Exercise 40: "Figure Eight/Vertical."

Exercise 41: "Triangle/Vertical."

Exercise 42: "Square/Vertical."

Exercise 43: "Triangle/Circle."

Exercise 44: "Triangle/Corkscrew."

Exercise 45: "Triangle/Figure Eight."

Exercise 46: "Square/Circle."

Exercise 47: "Square/Corkscrew."

Exercise 48: "Square/Figure Eight."

Exercise 49: "Circle/Horizontal (In Time)."** This exercise, and those which follow, are exactly the same designs and shapes as those above, done in a manner that seems metered or in time. Each linear or circular movement should happen in one beat of a steady tempo. By showing a lilting quality in every motion, your hands will look like the flowing, swaying motions of a ballroom dancer, effervescently performing a waltz. Here the hands should look very much in sync with each other, in a very musical, elegant, flowing manner.

Exercise 50: "Corkscrew/Horizontal (In Time)."

Exercise 51: "Triangle/Horizontal (In Time)."

Exercise 52: "Square/Horizontal (In Time)."

Exercise 53: "Circle/Vertical (In Time)."

Exercise 54: "Corkscrew/Vertical (In Time)."

Exercise 55: "Triangle/Vertical (In Time)."

Exercise 56: "Square/Vertical (In Time)."

Exercise 57: "Triangle/Circle (In Time)."

Exercise 58: "Triangle/Corkscrew (In Time)."

Exercise 59: "Square/Circle (In Time)."

Exercise 60: "Square/Corkscrew (In Time)."

Exercise 61: "Moving Spiral/Moving Spiral (Same Vertical Direction)." Picture a spring stretched vertically in length, each loop maintaining the same width as it spirals up. For this exercise both hands will start at their position of rest and move in a continually upward direction while looping in the same counterclockwise manner. Make certain every spiral motion stays the same width as it ascends. Continue the style of "in time," lilting motion from the previous exercises. Then, for this exercise as well as all of the following which use a spiral, repeat the exercise with the direction of the spirals now moving in mirror image, one clockwise and the other counterclockwise.

Exercise 62: "Moving Spiral/Moving Spiral (Opposite Vertical Direction)." For this exercise, one hand starts up in the air and spirals vertically downward as the other hand starts at your position of rest and spirals vertically upward.

Exercise 63: "Growing Spiral/Growing Spiral (Same Vertical Direction)." This is the same as Exercise 61, with both hands moving vertically up or down at the same time; however, the spirals start small and gradually increase in width to produce spirals which appear to grow in size.

Exercise 64: "Growing Spiral/Growing Spiral (Opposite Vertical Direction)." This is the same as Exercise 62, having one hand initially move upward as the other moves downward, now with growing spirals in both hands.

Exercise 65: "Growing Spiral/Moving Spiral (Same Vertical Direction)." For this exercise, both hands move vertically up or down at the same time; however, one hand moves in a growing spiral while the other simply creates a moving spiral.

Exercise 66: "Growing Spiral/Moving Spiral (Opposite Vertical Direction)." This is the same as the previous exercise, having one hand initially moving upward as the other moves downward; a growing spiral in one hand and a moving spiral in the other.

Exercise 67: "Triangle/Triangle (In Canon)." Starting up in the air, have both hands move diagonally down and to the left, then horizontally to the right, and finally diagonally up and to the left to create two same image triangles. Move in a lilting, metered style of one beat for each segment of the triangle.

After several cycles of that motion, when both hands arrive at the place they began, freeze the right hand while the left hand continues to move along one leg of its triangle. Both hands then continue from where they are, leaving the right hand trailing behind the left by one segment of a triangle. After a time, at a moment when the right hand arrives at what was its starting point, freeze it again while the left hand continues ahead one more segment of the triangle. Both hands then continue from where they are, staying two segments apart. After repeating this process one more time, both hands will be right back where they were at the start of the exercise.

Exercise 68: "Square/Square (In Canon)." This is the same as the previous exercise with the shape of squares in both hands.

Exercise 69: "Triangle Pointing Up/Triangle Pointing Down (Mirror Image)." From your position of rest, have your left hand move diagonally up and to the left, then diagonally down and to the left, and finally horizontally to the right creating the shape of the triangle used previously with its peak pointing up and its base moving horizontally at the level of your position of rest. At the same time, the right hand will move diagonally down and to the right, up and to the right, and finally horizontally to the left creating an upside-down version of the triangle being done in the left hand, with its peak pointing downward and its top segment moving horizontally at the level of your position of rest.

Exercise 70: "Triangle Pointing Up/Triangle Pointing Down (In Canon)." Using the design of the triangles in the previous exercise, repeat the process used in Exercise 67, freezing the right hand while the left hand moves along one segment at a time until both hands finally reach their starting point.

Conclusion

Freedom. A remarkable word that for a conductor comes from having confidence in his or her abilities. And for that, developing our physical skill is as important as developing our intellect. The greatest realizations, analyses and interpretations will be rendered lame if the conductor does not possess the physical skill to portray his or her intent.

But how wonderfully liberating it is to have the freedom to conduct what we want, how we want, when we want, with none of the apprehension caused by a lack of physical ability. It could be conducting beat patterns in the right hand while the left hand shows a horizontal line depicting almost stagnant inflection, or a wafting arc of sound emulating windchimes, or an okay sign offering praise to a student. That's freedom.

It is my hope that through exercises such as these we can each find those skills, and in so doing, the ability and confidence to paint any musical picture, describe any heartfelt emotion, and emulate any sound we can imagine. ▉

"But I'm Yelling as Nicely as I Can!"

There you are, standing on the podium in front of your one-hundred-member ensemble, rehearsing on the stage of the auditorium. From your perspective, it looks as though the percussion section is so far away as to be in the next county. From far left to far right seems to stretch a span the likes of the Golden Gate Bridge. All you can think is, "I'll have to virtually yell to be heard by all." We all know that a soft voice draws our performers' attention to us, and that talking over an ensemble is fruitless. However, the bottom line is that when we have a very large group, especially in a very large rehearsal space, even with ensembles that have been trained to be extremely quiet and attentive, our voice has to be heard. Nothing makes students tune us out faster than simply not being able to hear our instructions. So what do we do? We offer our comments at the loudest volume we can, trying to ensure that we are heard in every corner of the room. That is certainly an enviable pedagogical and practical goal.

The problem is at that volume we always sound angry. We sound as though we are yelling at them. Why? Because at a very loud volume it is extremely difficult to vary the inflection. Let's face it, at a normal voice, our variety of inflection and dynamic contrast is vast. At a constant shout, it has one setting: mad. Do we mean to sound that way? Absolutely not. Do our students know that? Absolutely not. That manner fosters an almost adversarial relationship. From the student's perspective, it sounds like we spend forty-two minutes of every forty-two minute rehearsal angry with them. At the very least, it doesn't allow us the freedom to use our voice with expression, sensitivity and nuance. We are too busy fighting to be heard. Are we exasperated? Probably not, but we sure sound it—all the time.

Now, if you are working with a moderate-sized group in a smaller space, the problem vanishes. But for those faced with this problem of being heard, it can be somewhat limiting if not debilitating. Not only does it take its toll on the tone of the rehearsal and the atmosphere in the room, it can be draining and physically dangerous for the teacher's voice. We have all heard stories of educators and the problems that have arisen after years of abuse to the vocal cords.

How do we fix the problem? Well, we can start simply by being conscious of the problem, and trying to use a kinder and gentler tone even at loud volumes. Also, with the problem in mind, we can force ourselves to use somewhat softer volumes so as to be able to vary the inflection and tenor of the communication. All too often we use more voice than is really necessary even for that big an ensemble in that big a room. By using those softer volumes we can begin to train our students to listen more intently.

If they are used to shouted directions, that is what they will listen for. It's just like watching television with the volume set very loud. We get used to it, even though we really don't need it set that high. Then if someone turns the television softer, at first it's hard for us to hear without really concentrating on the words. It may not be the volume is set too softly, just that we need to get used to the new "normal." As conductors, we can slowly reduce our speaking volume to a level that offers us more expressive flexibility, but is still understood by our students.

What do we do if that still doesn't help enough? I have taken to using a wireless lapel microphone, clipped onto my shirt collar, which goes through a small speaker. Placed on the side or in the back of the room, it serves to reinforce my voice, allowing me to use it as I would in a small room: with lots of variety of volume and inflection. I can whisper and be heard by all. I can have the most subtle lilt in my voice carry to every corner of the room. Systems like this one are very affordable and can make a great deal of difference. Is it a small extravagance? Maybe, but aren't you and your students worth it?

Again, I come back to Abraham Maslow's wisdom: if the only tool you have is a hammer, all of your problems start to look like nails. If the only "tool" with which we think we have to project is a loud voice, we will attempt to solve all of our "being-heard" problems as if they were "nails," with that ever-louder, perceived-as-angry voice. We can try to speak loudly as *nicely* as we can, but it still sounds like yelling if we're not very, very careful. A simple tape recording of our rehearsal can tell us how we sound to our students: not how we want to sound, but how we really sound. Try it; you may find yourself wondering, "Why does that conductor sound so mad?" We all preach to our students that what matters most when making music is the quality of their *tone*. Hmm…"what's good for the goose"…well, you know. ▪

FORTY-TWO STONES
AND AN EMPTY JAR

Ancient wisdom reminds us that today, this day, any day, is a gift. We can use it however we wish. But when it is over, it will be gone forever. We will have used it wisely or squandered it foolishly, but unquestionably we can never have it back again. All the more reason we should treasure every moment and savor its passing. Quite simply, we must cherish the promise of every new day.

To me, it's like an empty jar we get to fill as we see fit. Empty, it is full of promise. Ultimately, however, the value of the jar, like the day, is predicated on what we put in it. A sentiment as simple as it is profound, and all too often a lesson learned when the joys of youth have long passed. A lesson we can help teach our students in word and deed, remembering all the while the wonderful Spanish proverb that reminds us, "More things grow in the garden than the gardener sows." Many more things are learned in our classes, lessons and rehearsals than we set out to teach.

I like to think of rehearsals and classes in just that way. Each one an empty jar—full of promise—which we get to fill as we see fit. Forty-two minutes for us to give as a gift to our students. Forty-two stones we get to put into our empty jar. As each minute passes, we are putting one stone in the jar. It is up to us to make each one valuable, worthwhile, rewarding and meaningful. It is up to us to decide what we put into that jar. It is up to us to fulfill the promise of each rehearsal or class, and in so doing help to fulfill the promise of each new day for our students.

So the next time you start a class or rehearsal, picture an empty jar right next to you, and with the passing of every minute envision yourself placing one of those forty-two, or thirty, or ninety stones you are given into the jar, and choose wisely. Look into the eyes of those you teach and honor them, and our art, with every one. ◼

"When...?" or "When...!"

It's all in a word. Or in this case, an inflection. Simply changing the way we say that one little word can make all the difference in the world. It can make our communication with a student positive and hopeful, or negative and defeatist. Every time we use that word we set up two possibilities: one optimistic, the other pessimistic.

Frustration and fatigue often lead us to use the latter if we're not careful, taking us down the path of being a negative influence in the classroom. However, the former provides us with a reinforcing and reassuring approach which fosters a positive environment. Can't you just hear statements like: "When are you going to stop talking?" Contrast that with: "When you are quiet in rehearsals it is so terrific!" How about: "When are you going to remember it's a B-flat?" versus "When you get that B-flat it will be so beautiful!" Or, "When are you going to play that chord in tune?" as opposed to "When we play that chord better in-tune it will be wonderful!"

The word *why*, though grammatically part of a question, can be used just as powerfully, reflecting a positive or negative attitude. Which of the following comments would you rather hear from your conductor if you were playing or singing in the ensemble? "Why aren't you following me?" or "Why don't I try conducting that another way so it's easier for you to follow me?" "Why does that have to sound so ugly?" or "Why don't we try playing with our most beautiful tone quality?" "Why are you playing it so heavy and accented?" or "Why not try playing with a lighter touch?"

Every time we use either "when" or "why" we have the choice to be positive or negative. Every time we comment to the ensemble we can couch it in a pessimistic or optimistic way. It seems so simple. In theory we all know it is. However, in the heat of the moment, with emotions flowing and frustration rearing its ugly head, which do we reach for? We must remember the one that will motivate our students better, and inspire them to improve. The answer is simple; remembering is hard; always following through is sometimes tremendously difficult. But *when* we do, we are all better teachers for having done so.

ROUTINE CAN BE
COMFORTABLE—AND
DEADLY

I was sitting on an airplane, waiting to be de-iced; the airplane, that is. The flight attendant promptly turned on the automated preflight safety briefing. You know, the one describing rules and procedures in the event of an emergency. Flying as much as I do, I stopped listening to that *routine* lecture decades ago. What they do and say is set. It is pat. It is the exact same thing on every flight. No, I'm not minimizing its importance. In fact, if I am ever on a flight that has a catastrophe, I'm sure somewhere in my last thoughts will be, "What did they tell me to do?" Followed promptly by, "Why didn't I listen to those briefings more carefully!"

On this flight, however, partway through the first sentence of the briefing, the recording started to skip and repeat like an old vinyl record album stuck on the same word over and over. The flight attendant reset the announcement and tried again. It jammed at the same spot. She then tried three more times. Still not working, she resorted to the old-fashioned, now obsolete, speech over the intercom using a microphone. On this small

airplane, there was only one flight attendant and the only microphone was a telephone-like handset. Knowing what she had to
do, she opened her manual to the required speech, took a deep
breath and prepared to do it the old-fashioned way. She had
to read the announcement while holding the headset between
her head and shoulder, because she had to keep her hands free
to demonstrate the seatbelt, flotation device and oxygen mask.
Needless to say, it was pretty rough. With all the telephone holding and demonstrating, she stumbled over and over again with
the reading. She was fighting a losing battle to continually find
her place in the manual after each demonstration, all the while
trying to hold the phone in place.

After a few moments of dropping the phone and getting lost,
she decided to just plain "wing it" (no pun intended). She used
normal everyday language, and joked with us, rather than reciting
the pat text given so routinely by the automated system. It was
wonderful! I listened to every word. Was there anything really
different about the information we were given? No. Was the material better or more correct? Surely not. But because it was not the
routine, I glued my attention to her every word.

By now, you are probably wondering what this could possibly
have to do with teaching music. Let me try to explain with a story. A
few years back, a friend of mine who is a wonderful composer wrote
me with a story from when his now-adult son was in junior high
school. The composer told of going to hear his son's band concert.
Upon returning home, the son mentioned a particular piece that
was performed, commenting about how great the first half sounded
and how awful the second half sounded. My friend then asked his
son why he thought this was. To which the son replied, "You know,
Dad, where it got bad was when the bell rang every day," going on
to describe rehearsals that were the epitome of routine.

How did that happen? Well, picture an ensemble where each rehearsal begins exactly the same way every day: the teacher welcomes the students, then launches into a set, routine warm-up drill which is followed by the working through of each piece for an upcoming concert. Routine would allow for that ensemble to get to the same spot in a piece when the bell rang every day. You may be thinking this is a very isolated case. Sadly, I fear it may be more common than you think. Though this is certainly the extreme, many ensembles begin every rehearsal with a set warm-up routine.

This probably starts with a tuning note or two, followed by several scales, arpeggios and articulation exercises. After reading that list of warm-up activities, you are probably confused, wondering what could possibly be wrong with that material. The answer: nothing! The material is wonderful; it is the routine drill of playing through that litany every day, over and over again that is the problem. Picture the scene: every player mindlessly pounding out those exercises without thought; all of them worrying more about what they will be having for lunch than how they are performing. Often compounding this problem is a director distracted by a multitude of responsibilities. The routine nature of the session allows for that mindless mood.

The activity becomes more about banging down keys, valves and sticks than about improving performance. It is not the *what*, but the *how* that makes this unsound. Mindlessness negates concentration on tone quality, intonation, breathing, blend, balance, articulation or any of the other important concerns of a good warm-up session.

If we simply vary our routine, constantly use different material and attend to those activities with rigorous concentration, we will keep our rehearsals fresh and encourage students not to play "on autopilot." They will glue their attention on us the way I did on my distressed flight attendant, rather than tune out the way I do with those prerecorded announcements. Is it correct for me to ignore those recordings? No. Is it correct for students to mindlessly play those warm-up exercises? No. But human nature being what it is, we must provide an environment that encourages concentration and rigorous attention at every turn. As F. M. Alexander taught, "Change involves carrying out an activity against the habit of life."

Does anyone intend for the ensemble they conduct to go through its paces in this manner? Of course not; but the habit of rehearsal often leads to that scenario. Granted, repetition and drill can be useful and are an essential aspect of training. As well, a routine can help facilitate structure and provide comfort. However, if not watched carefully, that routine can become deadly to the concentration, attention and focus of performer and teacher alike. Somewhere, that flight attendant is traveling the skies. She probably hopes to forget that flight, not knowing I'll always remember it.

"Spoon-Feeding..."

Picture a scene: my mother and I having dinner at a wonderful five-star restaurant in New York City. We sit down to a lavish, gourmet meal served by waiters dressed in black tie and tails. After a lovely aperitif, our server brings us a breathtakingly beautiful tureen of crème de haricot verde. Ah! Our imagination runs wild with excited anticipation.

Then, at the moment we begin to eat, my mom starts spoon-feeding me this lovely repast. There I sit, with her feeding me a spoonful at a time; spoonful after spoonful. At the very least, that would be an odd sight. Anyone watching would certainly be puzzled. Seemingly able to eat on my own, why would I need to be spoon-fed?

Now, change scenes completely. Picture me and my mother having dinner at our home when I was one year old. There we were with a baby-food jar of pureed string beans, Mom dutifully spoon-feeding me. That scenario sounds perfectly normal, doesn't it? The *only* difference between those two scenes is forty-seven years.

That is the essence of a marvelous quote by E. M. Forster: "Spoon-feeding in the long run teaches us nothing but the shape of the spoon," the words "long run" being what's vitally important. We all would agree that at the start of a very young person's edu-

cational career and many times during "new" learning adventures
later in life, spoon-feeding is not only acceptable, it is necessary.

Whether it is due to a person's maturation level, inexperience,
discomfort or uneasiness, we may need to spoon-feed much information. It is, however, our constant effort to wean students away
from our spoon-feeding that makes all the difference. Just like my
mom did for me with those pureed string beans, we spoon-feed
our students so they get the nutrition they need, but then we
encourage them to hold the spoon, play with the jar, mess around
with the food, and in so doing, figure the whole thing out.

Can it be messy? Yes! Can pureed string beans end up on the
kitchen walls? Yes! But, what is the true purpose of education? Is it
simply achieving a goal? No! That goal or knowledge must foster
lifelong learning. We must teach them to *someday* be able to feed
themselves with that spoon; then with a fork, a knife, chopsticks,
and all other manner of feeding oneself. To borrow a sentiment
from my dear friend Reber Clark, "The challenge of education is
to make it point past itself." How incredibly true! It is only through
our ever-vigilant dedication to "teaching" our students *how to learn*,
and *how to teach themselves*, that our work will "point past itself."

Will that mean many moments of students trying to do something they find difficult? Would it often be easier to just spoon-
feed that material? Sure. But in the words of John Stuart Mill,
"The pupil who is never required to do what he cannot do, never
does what he can do." *Then*, and quite possibly forever. So put on
your apron, face mask and hip boots, and after you've spoon-fed
your students enough to be healthy and happy, help them to learn
how to feed themselves. Someday, when those very same students
are "savoring" the making of great music, they will remember who
taught them how to use that "spoon."

"IF YOU'VE TOLD A CHILD..."

On the great master list of what drives teachers crazy, certainly repetition would number in the top few. Repeating the same thing over and over again can be frustrating to say the least! Repeating the same thing over and over again can be frustrating to say the least! Repeating the same thing over and over again can be frustrating to say the least! (Sorry, I couldn't resist.)

I am not talking about the need for review or practice. I am referring to saying the same thing, time after time, trying to get a concept through to a student. For me, a simple test is whether I want to (though hopefully don't) start a comment with: "How many times do I have to tell you...!" That's the test. Something like: "Jimmy, (how many times do I have to tell you) accidentals carry through the entire measure!" Or, "Susan, (how many times do I have to tell you) to breathe correctly!" Need I go on?

Yes, sometimes a little repetition is what Jimmy and Susan need to remind them of what they already know. But all too often they don't remember because they really don't understand. Maybe they just need to learn it a different way. In the words of Walter Barbe as quoted by William Purkey, "If you've told a child a thousand times, and the child still has not learned, then it is not the child who is the slow learner." Sometimes, those "Eureka!" moments when a student finally "gets it" are a result of its finally making sense after many repetitions, but we often can expedite that process by simply changing the way we teach.

It may not be a matter of the glass being half empty or half full, it may just be *the wrong size glass!* We might need to get a glass that fits the situation. When we can't catch a mouse with a trap, we can keep setting the trap with the same cheese every time it fails, or we can spend time trying to figure out what kind of cheese he may like better. It is often easier, or maybe better put, a more natural instinct, for us to do it *again* rather than try to figure out a way to do it *better.*

THE INTERMITTENT
REHEARSAL

Of all the suggestions I have made in sessions and writings over the years, the one that has generated the most positive feedback from teachers is the use of occasional *silent rehearsals*. This is where the conductor says nothing. The titles of works to be rehearsed are on the board, rehearsal numbers are given by holding up fingers, rehearsal letters are indicated by preprinted three-by-five cards that are held up, and all other information is shown with the face, body and hands. This is the best way I know to force us to put our money where our hands are, rather than relying on our words to describe what we want.

As I have said before, without question there are times we must use words to teach or describe, but I believe all too often we "talk through" what could so much better be expressed nonverbally. This forces us to further develop our conducting to portray what we want by truly emulating sound in motion. It also fosters remarkable communication between ensemble and conductor, an extremely focused and disciplined environment, and artistic rewards words can't describe. It is my favorite way to energize a rehearsal and engage students in an almost mesmerizing fashion. It really does work wonders.

Another technique that works extremely well is what I call the *intermittent rehearsal*. For this, I verbally instruct students to start performing the passage being rehearsed as normal. Then when I clap, they are to continue "playing" silently by fingering, mouthing, bowing or sticking their parts—doing everything they normally would—except making a musical sound. They must also remain ready to return to playing the instant I clap again. In addition, for instrumental ensembles, I often have students sing or hum as they "play" silently.

While the students silently rehearse the piece, I conduct the composition as usual. I also mention key concepts or events in the music to reinforce what has been rehearsed. I point out what they "should" be doing at that moment, or key concepts that had been weak before, with short, terse statements such as *"crescendo," "forte"* or *"legato"* to remind them of their musical responsibilities.

A myriad of rehearsal possibilities are available to the conductor by having the ensemble alternate among normal playing, silent playing, singing/humming without silent playing, and singing/humming with silent playing, each done with or without the teacher talking through events while conducting.

This rehearsal technique has so many benefits. Students can focus on the technical aspects of playing without having to worry about sound production; concentrate on the conductor's gestures, now startlingly vivid in relative silence; have key musical events reinforced; and, most importantly, audiate, sing or hum their parts with the concomitant improvement in intonation. In addition, this technique works very well on the day of a performance, allowing rehearsal without embouchure fatigue.

Picture the focus and concentration of students rehearsing a composition starting with only the first measure played as normal, then four measures of silent playing, then four measures of singing while silently playing. All the while, the conductor draws attention to details of the work by mentioning reminders. How better to improve the tuning at a particular spot in a work than audiating and then singing it? How better to work out the technical demands of a passage than to concentrate on fingering it?

As long as the parameters of this type of rehearsing are ability-appropriate, and readiness is carefully considered, this technique can be used at any level for suitable lengths of time. Used well, this is a wonderful workout for the mind, fingers and ear. Does this replace normal rehearsals? Certainly not, but it does provide variety to our routine and focus on key aspects of performance.

Tomorrow, do five minutes of a *silent rehearsal* and another five minutes of an *intermittent rehearsal*. You will feel exhilarated. Your students will be drawn in by a vortex of concentration, awareness and challenge. All of you will further seal the bonds of communication and raise the bar of musical performance and understanding.

Sometimes what's needed isn't a new food to eat for dinner but simply a new way to prepare it. Sometimes what's needed isn't a new goal for our rehearsal but simply a new way to rehearse it. Try these two ways and then invent others that help make rehearsals as enjoyable as they are productive.

WHO'S RESPONSIBLE?

O f all the different philosophies, attitudes and concepts we deal with as music educators, I believe the one that fuels more disputes and garners the most controversy is that of player responsibility versus conductor responsibility for ensembles. The basic question is: who's responsible, the performers or the conductor? I have always been a strong advocate for conductor responsibility. I tell ensembles that if they are watching me, anything that goes wrong is my fault. My usual statement is that even if the building falls down, if they're looking at me, it's my fault! However, if they are staring at the fuzzy little black dots on the paper, they take all responsibility.

That philosophy is contrary to that of many who feel students must be made responsible for everything and that our purpose as conductor is to make ourselves unnecessary. Those conductors do not tell students how to execute a passage but rather ask for opinions to be discussed in rehearsals for almost every aspect of the piece. In that way, a group consensus decides every facet. Some believe a conductor should encourage students to listen *rather* than watch the conductor. Not listen *and* watch; listen, *not* watch. Those teachers fear students will not learn to make decisions if they are not solely responsible for making those decisions.

The answer, I believe, is that we must *teach students how to be responsible*, not simply *make them responsible*. To illustrate my point, let me ask you a question: who is responsible for *my* health? Is it my parents, my old pediatrician, my current physician or me? I think the answer is *"yes!"* All of those people at one time or another were responsible for my health. As an infant, I certainly had nothing to do with my own health. My pediatrician was primarily responsible, aided by my parents. As I got older, my parents took a more prominent role, though the pediatrician still had the final word. As a young adult, with the pediatrician now out of the picture, I had to take more and more responsibility for my own health, with my parents and doctor as advisors. Finally, as an adult, my health became my responsibility. It is true that my physician helps with the big decisions, but most of the responsibility falls squarely on my shoulders—as well it should.

As an infant, I knew nothing. As I grew older, I learned more and more about staying healthy. Between my pediatrician's wisdom and my parents' guidance, I slowly learned more and more about how to take care of myself. Fortunately, by the time I was an adult and needed to be responsible for myself, I was armed with enough information and guided experiences. I was indeed *ready* to be responsible. To me, that is exactly how ensembles should develop.

If as Michael Gorman states, "A student by definition is a person who doesn't know what he or she doesn't know," then we must take responsibility for musical decision-making as a way of training young people how to make those decisions. Leroy Anderson, when describing the art of composing and arranging, said it best: "Any ten-year-old can do this—with thirty years of training." Musical decisions, though occasionally "educated guesses," should be reasoned, learned opinions based on training and experience. Young people, by nature of their experience, are not equipped to be responsible for making those decisions. Without a background in music history, analysis, harmony, ear training, orchestration and the like, those decisions would rarely be more than "stabs in the dark."

In addition, notice I had one physician in my example. Oh sure, sometimes we have a few doctors helping us, but for the most part one person serves as our ultimate guide for that moment. If we have eighty players in an ensemble, we will get eighty opinions on how a piece should be performed. Ultimately, one person must make those decisions, or simple matters will become overly time-consuming, if not downright chaotic.

I believe the answer lies in the fact that we need to teach our students how to make musical decisions by *our making decisions* in rehearsals. They learn appropriate musical responses by their performing what we feel is appropriate, and our providing solutions and decisions about the music at hand, based on our learned opinion. They learn how to approach certain options by their watching the choices we make, and learning why we made them. They learn to be flexible by their seeing us change our minds. They learn that rarely is there only one "right" answer by their hearing us experiment. They learn to model good decisions by our example and training. However, this only works if we include our students in the process, rather than keep them at arms' length as to why we do what we do. In that way, making real the words of Oliver Wendell Holmes: "Man's mind stretched to a new idea never goes back to its original dimensions."

To start, our students must be taught they are *always* responsible for their own tone quality, posture, breath support, hand position, embouchure and all other individual playing concerns. Also, they must be taught to constantly monitor and be responsible for all aspects of how they contribute to matters of balance, blend, articulation and intonation. In addition, responsibility regarding the interpretation of solos should be given to students if they are ready for that role.

However, for all ensemble-decisions of interpretation, students must be taught how to make judgments. We must teach them about foreground and background by showing them which aspects of a piece should be brought out, such as melodies, countermelodies, passing tones and suspensions, versus what should be kept in the shadows. We must teach them why certain tempos, articulations, balances, phrasing, dynamics, melodic contours, liberties or strictures are appropriate and why others are not. Indeed, we must train them about those choices, and all musical decisions, as sure as we teach them correct posture and hand position.

After they have learned enough information to begin to make informed choices, we should allow for guided decision making. This can be fostered by situations where we have the ensemble try a passage two different ways. Then we guide them through the process of how to make a reasoned decision. We also can start to ask specific students their opinions about choice of mallets, articulation, dynamics, phrase peaks or anything else, and contrast those to our own. Slowly, we will force them to start making choices on their own with the "safety net" of our guidance under them.

The most significant step in the process of getting them to "test their wings" is through solo and chamber music opportunities. Here they can take what they have learned in the quasi-dictatorial large ensemble rehearsal, whether from instruction or guided response, and assert their own ideas, listen to peer colleagues' opinions, experiment, and ultimately make reasoned, learned decisions on their own.

"If you put a plant in a jar, it will take the shape of the jar. But, if you allow the plant to grow freely, twenty jars might not be able to hold it." Those words of Mike Krzyzewski are so true, but the given in that sentiment is the plant must be well-planted, nurtured and ready to sprout before being allowed to grow freely. That's what we must do for our students.

So who's responsible? We are. We need to train them how to play, what to play, and when to play, by developing our conducting to be truly communicative, functionally and impressionistically. Then, once we have *taught* them to watch in rehearsals, we can be in control and affect musical decisions as we wish. However, we are also responsible for the *why*. That is where we teach them musical judgment based on intelligent decisions.

There are certainly times we will want to have them play without us at the podium, those moments forcing them to listen more than watch, and to learn they can play without our help. However, we should always possess the control to get their attention—get them to watch—at any given moment so we can fix or change anything in an instant. But if we give up responsibility, and thus control of the ensemble, we won't be able to help if they get into trouble. If their playing starts to phase and come unglued, our students may not hear it until it is too late. We *can* hear it and, if we are in control, fix it while it is still fixable. As Publilius Syrus warned, "Anyone can hold the helm when the sea is calm."

As well, our students' perspectives of how something sounds, depending on where they sit, may be very different than what should be portrayed. Only *we* have the vantage point to assess that, let alone the ability to correct for it as it happens. In addition, we must be the one to raise the bar of excellence. The students in our ensemble don't know how good they should be or can be; teaching them *that* is our responsibility. I think of the whole matter in terms of the fabulous statement adapted from the words of Louis Nizer: "When a man points a finger at someone else, he should remember that three of his fingers are pointing at himself." When we "point" to students to tell them their ensemble's performance is their responsibility, we must keep in mind that *three times the number of fingers* are aiming that responsibility right back toward us.

Let us not forget that for those given great opportunity comes great responsibility. I once saw a cartoon that said: "Being the grown-up stinks, because it comes with all that responsibility." So true. But if *we* don't, *they* can't. ■

"THE GOAL IS *NOT* TO BE UNDERSTOOD"

What is the goal of a great communicator? The answer to that question has so many facets it would take volumes to do it justice. However, wouldn't you agree *getting the point across—* whatever that is—has to number high on the list? If so, that goal could simply be stated as *being understood.* In other words, people *understood* what was being communicated; the communicator's intentions were *understood.* And what is a writer, speaker, teacher or conductor, but a communicator? So being understood must be our goal. Right? Well, yes and no. Being understood is only part of the answer. Great communicators know they must go much further than that.

There is a wonderful old joke about a man parachuting from a burning airplane only to land in the middle of a massive, sprawling corn field in the heart of Iowa. As the man sits on the ground in a state of panic, trying to figure out what to do, he sees a person riding a bicycle along a road in the distance. Excitedly, the stranded man jumps up and yells to the bicycler, "Where am I?" To which came the answer, "In the middle of a cornfield." The information in the reply was perfectly correct, but equally and totally useless.

The bicyclist gave a clear and meaningful answer that *was understood* by the stranded man. The problem was the man on the bike simply didn't know his audience.

As Stephen R. Covey wrote, we must "Seek first to understand, then to be understood." If our well-meaning bicycler had simply taken the time to come to know the background and situation of the person asking the question, he would have been able to offer a response that was as useful as it was understandable. As farfetched as this story is, it does point to the source of a great deal of frustration for teacher and student alike. The most well-intentioned, thought-out, and expertly taught material is worthless to students who are not ready or able to receive it. If they do not possess the mental, physical or emotional readiness to learn what is being taught, it will not be understood, frustrating teachers who are trying their best to teach as much as the students who are trying their best to learn. The problem is often not that we taught it poorly, or we were *not* understood, but because *we simply didn't understand* our audience. The better we understand our students, the better we can plan, sequence, prepare and teach material that can—and thus will—be learned. Whether it's a physical technique, an intellectual concept or an emotional perception being taught, understanding who our students are and where they came from is as important as where we want them to go. Assessing the situation, and understanding *them*, becomes far more important than being understood. Great communicators know that, but also know they must go further still.

Nearly two thousand years ago there lived a philosopher by the name of Epictetus. Though he lived most of his life in the first century A.D., it is amazing that his wisdom regarding this matter is as profound today as it was then. Wisdom—true wisdom—seems only to get better, or at least truer, with age. He cautioned, "Do not write so that you can be understood, write so that you cannot be misunderstood." A more perfect goal I can't imagine.

As teachers, how many of us have taught something *we* were sure our students understood? More importantly, something *our students* were sure they understood? Then upon evaluation we come to realize they didn't "get it" at all. Was it that they didn't understand? Sometimes, yes. But I believe it's far more likely that they *misunderstood*. Thinking of the advice of Epictetus, we probably taught the material so we were understood, *but not* so we couldn't be *misunderstood*. We knew what we wanted them to learn, but did they? Well, they thought they did. But sometimes, *what they understood* just wasn't *what we meant them to understand*.

It could have been the words we used as part of our instructions, which our students took to mean something different from which we meant; physical gestures we made to emulate sounds, which they took as something very different from what we intended; or body language and facial expressions they read far differently from what we wished to imply. All these are simple misunderstandings. Scowls on our faces, complete with furrowed-brows that come about from our focused listening to a passage or from intense concentration, can be misunderstood to mean disappointment or frustration. A conductor's loud voice can be misunderstood as communicating frustration, when it could be honest excitement and enthusiasm.

So perhaps our goal should be *first to understand*, and then to make certain we *can't be misunderstood*. Once we understand our students, we must not just teach and conduct so we can be understood, but rather teach and conduct so we cannot be misunderstood. Though that might sound like a game of semantics, it can make all the difference in the world. A difference Epictetus certainly understood. ▨

EXCELLENCE

What is excellence? How do you define that profound ideal? When I think of excellence—true excellence—I think of the drive to do more than what is required, to do better than what is needed, and to go further than what is necessary. Not for the praise of others, but simply because our inner values, pride in our work, and willingness to go above and beyond dictate nothing less. And what always comes to mind is that magnificent "Lady" that adorns the New York City Harbor.

Seeing the Statue of Liberty from the ground or from the water is a grand and magnificent sight. One cannot help but to be struck with the beauty and power of the sculpture. The craftsmanship and detail of every facet of her crown, body, gown and face are truly remarkable. How can one look at her and not think the word "excellence?" However, flying down the Hudson River in an airplane or helicopter, soaring five hundred feet above that incredible monument, you see the *true* excellence of Lady Liberty.

From that vantage point, looking down on her head, you will see that every wisp, curl and strand of hair, as well as the back of her crown, was painstakingly fashioned to perfection. Every feature of that portion of the statue is as stunning—every detail as profound—as the rest. Think of the hours of work that went

into those remote areas. At first glance, it is easy to think of that as
simply a reflection of the *talents* of the sculptor, Frederic Auguste
Bartholdi. Well, it is far more than that! For you see, as far as he
could have known, no one would ever see the top of the Statue of
Liberty. No one.

Why? Because on October 28, 1886, when the great statue
was dedicated by President Grover Cleveland, Orville and Wil-
bur Wright would still be seventeen years away from their his-
toric flight of December 17, 1903. Though it's true the Mongolfier
brothers had invented their hot air balloon some one hundred
years before the Statue was made, realistically, Bartholdi probably
thought only stray seagulls and pigeons would ever be the ben-
eficiary of the exceptional efforts made to fashion the top of her
head. In his mind, who would ever be able to look down on the
statue from above to see the majesty of his work?

The sculptors, having no way of knowing that anyone would
ever soar above their creation, still made the effort—gave of
themselves—to make even those parts that would never be seen
by any living soul, other than themselves, as beautiful and perfect
as the rest. Why? Because their dedication to their craft allowed
them to do nothing less. They sought not the adulation of others,
but the *inner* knowledge that *they* gave their best effort, that their
artistic pursuit was done as well as possible for no other reason
than great art demanded it. Is that not the very definition of excellence? Is that not art for art's sake? Is that not the essence of quality and taking pride in one's work?

Pushing ourselves and our students to understand, or, better
put, having our students *come to understand* that simple thought,
may be more important than anything we teach. What better gift
can we give than sending all of our students off with that sense of
integrity for their art, work and lives? Searching for the smallest

detail in the big picture may mean the difference between good and great. Work, even on seemingly insignificant minutia, may be the path to true excellence. As the great architect Ludwig Mies van der Rohe stated so eloquently, "God is in the details."

I also think of excellence in terms of what has become known as the "Butterfly Effect" theory of chaos, first put forth by Edward Lorenz. This concept is best known by the simple question he posed: "Does the flap of a butterfly's wings in Brazil set off a tornado in Texas?" The premise is that even the smallest detail or event, viewed individually as seemingly insignificant or random, can compound and in that way magnify and contribute to a much greater, even profoundly powerful outcome.

An almost imperceptible happening can be the start of a pattern or string of events—one "feeding" off of or made possible by another—that can end up having great impact. I don't really know if the flap of a butterfly's wings in South America *can* cause a Tornado in Texas, but I do know that the performance of even the smallest musical subtlety can sometimes be the spark that starts a chain of ever-intensifying focused and impassioned music-making.

As one small impulse by a snake contributes to propel that animal through its serpentine movements, our attention to the details of our craft and our students' performance helps propel our students to reach their potentials, and the composition to fulfill its communication.

The "what" of excellence—exemplified by those tiny details of The Lady of the Harbor which make her so perfect—coupled with the "why" of excellence—explained by "The Butterfly Effect" of how events can compound to become extremely powerful—reflect my belief that even the smallest detail of our interpreting, conducting and rehearsing a work, and our students attention to and execution of those details, matter greatly. They matter profoundly.

The more details we discover from studying a work, the more we can attend to in our conducting and rehearsing. The more we attend to in our conducting and rehearsing, the more our students can bring the piece to life. Ostensibly small details, such as a single suspension, accent, passing tone or lilting phrase could be the nuance that makes for a performance of excellence. Not simply because of the attention to detail beyond the obvious, but because those events can be the catalyst for a chain of ever-increasingly powerful expression.

A detail as small as "leaning on" one specific tone in a phrase to provide a moment of unexpected or heightened tension can be the spark that energizes an expressive contour toward a remarkable musical goal. One intense accent amidst a sea of legato sounds may offer a vehicle for increased energy and momentum. A subtle slackening of tempo may permit a moment of repose which will allow an even more astonishing climax to follow.

Why? Why such concern over those smallest of nuances? Because we don't know what detail or subtlety will cause a tear to fall on the faces of our young musicians, or a chill up the spine, or that unexplainable tingle at the core of our being. What tiny, possibly unnoticed sound will be the start of building emotions that will reach extraordinary proportions? No one knows; that's why each and every one is so important.

Excellence, therefore, must be heard in the obvious, but possibly more important, in the barely perceptible. There is no doubt that the creation or performance of great art, and for that matter great "anything" in life, comes down to a simple phrase that reminds us that, "Countless unseen details are often the only difference between mediocre and magnificent."

True excellence is attending to every detail, no matter how small or "unseen," because our commitment to our art will allow nothing less. True excellence knows that those details can compound to create a "tornado" of impassioned performance. Education, in many ways, can be thought of as passing on to future generations the gift of knowing excellence, striving for excellence, appreciating excellence and living excellence. How magnificent!

THE FLAMES OF
GROWTH

I t is said that "Genius is the fire that lights itself." Well, I don't
know about that, but I do believe that *learning* is *the fire that lights
itself.* Finding excitement at the thought of *not* knowing, being curious as to how or why, having a willingness to take educational
risks, believing in oneself and growing from mistakes is indeed
a fire that lights itself. Simple curiosity starts a smoldering ash
which grows into a fire that is *knowing more.*

Isn't that true learning? Isn't that what each of us wants our students
to come to know? Of course we want to help them learn facts; education requires a certain amount of that. But, of greater worth, don't we
want to give them a foundation—a burning desire—for learning?
Don't we want them to learn to *want to learn*, learn *to learn*, and come
to realize that the *pursuit* of knowledge and ability starts with not just
admitting, but relishing the thought of not having an answer?

"I Don't Know."

I was recently teaching a graduate seminar course at the university. During one specific class, after I had just finished giving

each student a topic to research for the next class, one of the students posed a question related to something we had discussed earlier that night. I was stymied—truly baffled. After thinking for a minute, I admitted my ignorance and told the class I now had *my* homework. And I guess as I said it my enthusiasm for learning must have shown. As my students saw their teacher thrilled at the joy of not knowing, one of them said, "Look at you all excited!" I was. I was truly beaming. Three little words set me on my way. Just like the saying goes, "All learning begins with the simple phrase, 'I don't know.'" Or as Socrates stated so clearly, "Wisdom begins in wonder."

That reminds me of a story. Years ago, a friend of mine stood for his doctoral oral exams. He sat in a room filled with professors from many disciplines. One after another, these learned scholars fired questions designed to challenge my friend's knowledge. All, that is, but one teacher, who just sat there listening. He said nothing and asked nothing. Finally, after all the teachers were satisfied, the committee chair asked if anyone had anything further. My friend saw light at the end of the tunnel when out of the blue that silent professor announced he had one question. He looked my friend in the eyes and said, "Tell me about John Irving Gemini III, listing his greatest accomplishments in order of importance."

My friend said his heart fell to the pit of his stomach as fear and trepidation flowed through his being. Not only did my friend not know the man's accomplishments in order of importance, he had never even heard of him. At that moment, my friend thought about trying to—how should I say—make something up, but thought better of it. Instead, he reflected a minute and proceeded to admit, sadly, that he did not know of the gentleman or his contributions. "But," he went on to say, "by the time the sun sets tonight, I will know everything there is to know about him and here's how," whereupon he stated, chapter and verse, how he would research the information.

The professor listened patiently, then responded by saying, "A rather good answer given the fact I made him up five minutes ago." After the inquisition (I mean orals) were over, my friend cornered the professor, asking why he did what he did. The response was as profound as the question was calculated: "With as much as you know," he said, "I just wanted to make certain you learned the most important lesson: saying 'I don't know.'" In the words of Chuang Tzu, "He who knows he is confused is not in the worst confusion."

"The ancestor of every action is a thought," Ralph Waldo Emerson tells us. It is simply a matter of whether we seize, and act upon, those thoughts that are fertile questions, and do so with delight. Roger Lewin said, "Too often we give children answers to remember rather than problems to solve." Certainly, we must do some of both, but don't you agree the answers we get through our own *endeavors of curiosity* become some of the most precious answers we learn? Getting students to perceive questions, to rejoice in the fact they *don't* have the answers, and to be equipped with the necessary tools for discovery, must number among the greatest gifts a teacher can give. Relishing in having the answer is one thing; relishing in *not* having the answer may be even better.

Believing in Themselves

James Russell Lowell asserted that "More men fail through ignorance of strength than through knowledge of their weakness." That is probably true, but I would contend even more people fail from a *lack of confidence* in their ability than through ignorance of strengths. In the words of Ralph Hodgson, "Some things have to be believed to be seen."

To that end, we must help instill that confidence *in our students,* getting them to truly believe in themselves. Telling them *we* have confidence in them is a first step. But "putting our money where our mouth is" by acting on that confidence is of even greater value. Giving students musical and organizational responsibilities, decisions to make, and tasks to perform goes a long way toward voting our confidence.

If that confidence is not instilled, the "knowledge of weakness" from the quote above quickly and firmly can become a conviction. Students then start to believe in their weaknesses more than their abilities to overcome them. They will, quite sadly, live the words of Richard Bach: "Argue for your limitations, and you get to keep them."

Take Risks Rather than Play it Safe.

"The greatest mistake you can make in life," warns Elbert Hubbard, "is to be continually fearing you will make one." Have truer words ever been spoken? How sad is it to see people, especially young people, so worried about making a mistake that they never put themselves in a position to make one. And by so doing, rarely taste failure, but virtually doom themselves to horizons that are in close reach. To be so afraid of mistakes that one becomes educationally frozen—paralyzed by fear—is debilitating to say the least. As David Grayson states, "We fail more often by timidity than by over-daring."

How noble is the goal of helping every student understand Frederick B. Wilcox's advice: "Progress always involves risks. You can't steal second base and keep your foot on first." Or André Gide's version of the same sentiment: "One does not discover new lands without consenting to lose sight of the shore for a very long time." It comes down to realizing, as James Thurber says, "You might as well fall flat on your face as lean over too far backward." But the thought which most profoundly describes the realization I hope each of my students comes to know is from Soren Kierkegaard: "To dare is to lose one's footing momentarily. Not to dare is to lose oneself."

Is it scary to put yourself out on a limb? Yes, but as Frank Scully questions, "Why not go out on a limb? Isn't that where the fruit is?" But James Bryant Conant may have summed it up most elementally: "Behold the turtle. He makes progress only when he sticks his neck out." I want only to ask every student and every teacher one question, posed by Robert H. Schuller: "What great thing would you attempt if you knew you could not fail?" How liberating it is to know the value of educational risk, be willing to take those risks, and derive pleasure in taking them.

Learn from Mistakes

"Failure is success if we learn from it," says Malcolm S. Forbes. Indeed. The joy of making mistakes is in learning from them, growing as a result of information gained from those mistakes. We must help students to grow and develop *from* mistakes, not *in spite* of them. With our guidance they will value what they learn from attempts that don't work as much as from those that do. It's simple: "Take risks: if you win, you will be happy; if you lose, you will be wise." To me, what fans that "fire" of education was best proclaimed by the remarkable Pablo Picasso when he humbly affirmed, "I am always doing that which I cannot do, in order that I may learn how to do it."

Then Risk Again

Armed with information gleaned from our mistakes, we must be willing—no, excited—to risk again, and again and again, learning more with every attempt. In that way the cycle of growth continues ever further. But to what end? What is the goal? Well, I think H. Jackson Brown, Jr. said it best: "A successful life doesn't require that we've done the best, but that we've done our best."

How powerful three little words can be. Three little words that can change a life. Three little words that can change the world—or at least our tiny part of it. Three little words that hold the key to learning. So every time you have helped a student to say or think those words—"I don't know"—realize you were the flint for their steel, that made a spark, that lit a fire of learning. The fire of learning that lights itself.

"But This is Only a Rehearsal!"

I don't think I have ever had a student say those words to me. But—worse—I have had many students perform in rehearsals as if they were thinking those words. If I were to list, in order, the top fifty frustrations I have had as a conductor and teacher over the years, numbers one through fifty would be just that. It drives me crazy when I look into faces and see young people giving half-heartedly of their abilities, concentration, emotions or determination. I don't understand it.

Why don't they all want to seize every single moment of rehearsal as an opportunity to passionately express themselves musically? Why don't they want to push the envelope of what they can achieve, feel and think, ending every rehearsal mentally, physically and emotionally exhausted? If I don't finish a rehearsal feeling drained, I know I didn't give my all; I just want *them* to do the same. Now when I am in the throes of rehearsal rapture, frenzy or elation I know my students think I take my job a bit too seriously. And I have had more than a few tell me, "You *have* to get a life!" But they eventually realize this is an important part of my life, and sharing my passion for it is part of me. Those rehearsals are far more important to me than any concert could ever be—for rehearsals are when I can be a teacher. I think that is when each of us can be the best we can be.

I have always found it interesting that even the great Arturo Toscanini was described by many who played for him as always at his best in rehearsals. They would often say he was good in concert, but he was great in rehearsals; that was where he truly shined. Fred Zimmerman recalled Toscanini's words: "'We have an obligation. *I* have it; *you* have it.' It was an obligation to the composer, to the music; they were of primary importance; only they mattered. And this obligation must be fulfilled always. I remember someone getting impatient and saying: 'But this is only a rehearsal!' 'Only a rehearsal!' said Toscanini. 'This is where we play for ourselves! *Now* we play, not tomorrow night!'" Of Toscanini, Hugo Burghauser wrote, "This creates such concentration and awe that people achieve beyond their usual capacity—not because they want to, but because they are elevated spiritually."

So why do kids sometimes play or sing like they don't care? I think the answer rests with my favorite saying about everything in education: "Kids can do anything; we just have to teach them how." We need to teach them *why* they need to care, *what* to listen for so they hear the fruits of their labor and *how* their efforts in rehearsal make all the difference.

But the truth is that we really can't tell them or lecture them. We simply need to have our enthusiasm, intensity, work ethic, sense of urgency, excitement, focus, energy, high expectations and willingness to show extremes of emotion, become contagious. In that way we will help students to make every musical moment count in rehearsals, "...where we play for ourselves." If the watershed moments of a student's music education are limited to performances, they will be few and far between. If those moments occur in rehearsals they will be many and often. ▧

"THE VIEW FROM THE MOUNTAINTOP"

There I sat, looking at my computer screen while tears came down my face. It was the night after a performance with the University Symphonic Band, and I had just received an email from one of my students, a wonderful person and a remarkable percussionist. In that, her senior year, she was one of those percussionists who knew what I wanted before I did and just never seemed to make a mistake. She was a gem in every way. I will never forget the words she wrote: "I need to thank you for never allowing me to be satisfied with less than what I am capable of; for never allowing me to cheat myself out of knowing exactly what my personal best is; and for keeping me reminded of why I chose this path in the first place."

That email was even more special than you might think; let me try to explain why by going back in time three years before it arrived. I can remember as if it were yesterday being in rehearsal with that same young lady, then a freshman percussionist I reluctantly let into the ensemble. I can flash back to rehearsals where I was frustrated to say the least. Quite frankly, early on, there were times when it was a good thing I had no hair, because I would have pulled it out.

Deep down I knew she wanted to be a fine percussionist. The truth is she motivated herself; I only watched and smiled. But I did try to push her ever further and to encourage her to believe in the power of her dreams. And day by day, with hard work, dedication and commitment, she surpassed even my wildest dreams in a precious few years.

In our own way, we each help our students to progress. My goal has always been that what *they now know* is what *they once never imagined*. Striving for ever-higher goals is like the view of a mountaintop from the ground below. Standing at the foot of a mountain, the only view is that peak you are trying to reach. It seems to be the only goal, so we work hard to get there. Only after we reach that summit do we see the top of an even higher mountain that now seems to have the highest peak. We work to get to that zenith, only to see one still higher. The funny thing is at the base of any mountain, its peak seems to be the loftiest height. It is *only* the view from the mountaintop that allows us to see the next even-higher place.

We must remember—and our students must learn the lesson—that we can never see what goals lie ahead. We can only work to reach our goals one summit at a time, knowing all the while we will go even farther than we can now fathom. How high will we, or our students, eventually reach? Who knows? As Pumbaa the lovable warthog queried in the movie *Lion King* 1½, "But, if you always go beyond what you see, how do you know when you're there?" You don't! However, as long as we all enjoy the journey, it will be worth every moment of it. We each strive for the best from ourselves and our students: one step at a time; one hill at a time; one mountaintop at a time.

I hope we can all push our students, and ourselves, never to settle for getting to the top of one mountain, to always look for the next peak. The trick is to remember to enjoy the view from the top of even the smallest hill and savor the beauty of that success. I share that email with you because it is what each of your students wants to say to you. The next time you look into the eyes of your students, know they thank you for never allowing them to be satisfied with less than what *they* are capable of; for never allowing them to cheat themselves out of knowing exactly what *their* personal bests are. They may rarely express it, but know they will *always* appreciate it. ■

"NOT AGAIN—BETTER"

L et's do that again." "One more time." "Play that again." "Could we try that again?" "How about we run that again?" How many times in any given rehearsal do we use phrases like those? Probably more than any of us would wish to count. But do we *really* mean "again"? Of course not. What we mean—to me the single most difficult idea to instill in students—is that every time we repeat something, the purpose is to improve upon it, not simply redo it. I know that seems extraordinarily obvious, but is it obvious to our students? And, even if it is, do they always act on it that way? How do we better instill that work ethic?

I think the first step is to make certain we always help our students understand *what* needs to be improved. In other words, why we are repeating the material. We have all been in rehearsals in which the conductor continually asks for a passage to be repeated without ever sharing with performers *why*. Without a doubt, if the performers don't know what's wrong they cannot possibly correct it. I don't think we do this intentionally, but in the heat of rehearsing, with our minds going a million miles an hour, that communication is often lost as a casualty of rapid pace or simple fatigue.

The second step is ensuring we always offer information on *how* to improve the performance, being as specific as possible. Not just *what* is wrong, but *how* to fix it. What technique could we suggest to remedy a problem? What could they *try* to improve a given ensemble concept? Armed with specific information about what is wrong and what they can do to improve, our students have the tools to improve *every time* we ask for a passage to be repeated. Of course, sometimes we repeat a section with no specific problem at hand, simply to improve cohesiveness, blend, expression or the like. In those cases, no specific problem is apparent, nor is any specific cure; the repetition is simply a means to better each student's sense of ensemble and the group's collective musical portrayal. That needs to be made clear to students, allowing them to understand *why* they are repeating something, so they know what to improve on.

The third step is for us to inspire students to develop a work ethic in which *they demand improvement from themselves* every time a passage is repeated. Through intense, focused rehearsals we can show them how important the work at hand is, how nothing but their best efforts are good enough, how beautiful their achievements are, that extraordinary concentration is a given, that every repetition offers an opportunity for growth, and that we will constantly "raise the bar" of our expectations. We must model that standard, showing by our words and deeds that we not only talk the talk, but walk the walk.

There is one story I tell every ensemble I have ever conducted. To me it represents all we seek from them and ourselves. Many years ago, I was told about a dress rehearsal of the legendary Arturo Toscanini conducting the NBC Symphony Orchestra. After many hours of intense work (and with Toscanini that is probably an understatement!), he was about to run through a composition they had all played many times before. Just before they began, he looked at the orchestra and firmly said, "Not again—better."

Here was one of the greatest conductors of all time rehearsing one of the most remarkable orchestras ever assembled, and he felt the need to remind *even them* that every time they played something it had to be better than the time before. I tell my students that if that great conductor had to remind those amazing performers of this simple goal, we could not be served better than never to forget its power. We ensure continuous improvement when we never settle for *again*, but always seek for *better*.

Another story I love to tell my students to further drive this point home was told to me by a music teacher I met while speaking in Los Angeles. She spoke of a concert she attended by the remarkable Itzhak Perlman at Walt Disney Hall in Los Angeles on January 8, 2005. Her eyes lit up as she talked about this fabulous performance of music for violin and piano. In the middle of the concert, however, while Mr. Perlman was performing Beethoven's "Kreutzer" Sonata, an alarm went off throughout the hall. The sound was startling, sending some to move toward exit doors, while others, stayed in their chairs.

After a few anxious moments, the alarm finally went silent, allowing all to return to their seats. Before he began to play after this forced respite, Mr. Perlman said to the audience, "That was Beethoven. He said, 'Play better.'" How profound. How perfectly profound. I know he was simply trying to put his audience at ease after a scare, but I am sure no one can get to be an Itzhak Perlman without truly thinking that way all the time. Each time I hear this great master perform, I feel as though he is playing with a thought such as that in mind.

So every time I rehearse a work, especially running through it during a dress rehearsal, I ask my students to remember those lessons taught by Toscanini and Perlman and not just play it again, but strive each time to play it better.

"A Ship in Port is Safe..."

I am blessed with wonderful students. The joy they bring me in rehearsals is immeasurable. We work very hard, though usually they put more pressure on themselves then I ever could. They are dedicated to doing their best for themselves, their peers, and most of all, for the music. You know what's so wonderful about being a music teacher? Every one of you would say the same thing about your own students!

Part of the joy is watching them as they play. Their faces are filled with so much expression. They each tell a story with every glance. Usually, I see wonderful faces filled with power, grace, confidence, intensity and pride. Sure, sometimes I do see the look of frustration or fatigue in their eyes. But usually the expressions remind me why I wouldn't want to do anything else in the world for a living.

I'd like to tell you about one time it *didn't* go that way. It happened one day during an honors band festival. We had been rehearsing for several hours and all was going fantastically well. The students were a delight in every way. At one point, we started working on a lush, romantically expressive work that allowed them to speak from their hearts. And that is exactly what they did. Since technique was less of a concern in this composition, they savored every phrase and showed it on their faces—faces that beamed.

As the rehearsal went on, we came to a very soft and delicate passage that had the principal trumpet player enter the sparse texture on a B-flat above the staff, creeping in with the softest of volumes and smoothest of articulations. Needless to say, this was a daunting task. After the principal player attempted it a few times, I asked the assistant principal player to give it a try, thinking she may be able to perform the passage even better. There was no fanfare, no histrionics, I simply wanted to hear a few of the possibilities before choosing who I thought was best suited to the task. Because I caught that young lady by surprise she had no time to hesitate. We started the passage, she came in beautifully, everyone "shuffled" in applause for her, I grinned in wonder—we had found the person. Or so I thought.

Looking at the trumpets, I said, "Both of you play it so well; it's hard to pick." Then, looking at the assistant principal player, I went on to say, "But would you play it?" At that second I saw a look no words could explain, a look best described as panic. I mean real panic. This young lady, who for half a day had the most wonderful look of enjoyment and joy, now had the look of a person in crisis. Instantly, the up-until-now-ever-present smile was gone as the color drained from her face. Seeing this, I offered words of praise for her exceptional performance and expressions of confidence in her ability. Well, that made *one* of us!

At the next break, that young lady came to speak to me privately. In the most polite and mature manner, she said, "Dr. Boonshaft, I think you should know that I have a history with that piece." I asked her what she meant. She went on to tell me that during the previous year she was the principal trumpet player of her All-State Band in which they performed the very same piece. She described how "that spot" went perfectly in *every* rehearsal. However, during the concert it was a disaster. As she recalled the event, the look on her face was so very sad. Every playing was wonderful but the last one, and that was a hard memory for her to take. Though she was willing to do what I asked, it was obvious she did not want to live that story out yet again.

At that moment, my thoughts turned to a remarkable quote by Admiral Grace Hopper: "A ship in port is safe, but that's not what ships are built for." So, I looked her in the eyes, and told her we had two choices. The first, and easiest, was for me to give her part to someone else. The second was for her to overcome her fear and to play the part; this was her chance to play it as beautifully as we both knew she could. I went on about how concerts don't matter and that rehearsals are where we grow as musicians, but nothing I said really helped. I told her I had all the confidence in the world in her and she needed to do the same. She needed to take this as an opportunity rather than a crisis. She understood, but that didn't make it any easier.

I could not allow that one bad moment to stay with her another second. I went on to say, "Since I *won't* do the first option, we better work on the second." I did fear what would happen if this time were like the last, but I could see in her eyes that it wouldn't be. I believed in my heart the risks of her trying were far less than the permanency of her not trying. She accepted my decision, though it was certainly not with enthusiasm.

Later in the day, we went back to work on that piece. Each time she played the passage more beautifully than the time before. She played like the most confident of professionals. The next morning, I told her how proud I was of her, and that now, since she had overcome her fear, I would let *her* decide whether she would play the part or not in the concert. Though her answer was still far from enthusiastic, she decided to continue on. As you could guess, she looked as if she were going to be ill each and every time we rehearsed that spot.

The performance was upon us. To tell the truth, I don't know which one of us was more nervous. Just before that spot, I looked her in the eyes, gave her a knowing grin of confidence and smiled as hard as I could. As I cued her, she played the passage as if guided by angels. It was magnificent. She played the performance better than ever. In the seconds just after she played—played like never before—I looked at her, smiled and nodded up and down as I closed my eyes to slow the tears. She didn't just play it, or play it well; she rose to heights no demon memory could withstand.

Yes, it was a risk. Yes, it could have gone horribly wrong. But from the moment she came to talk with me, all I could think of was the remarkable quote by Saul David Alinsky: "When written in Chinese, the word 'crisis' is composed of two characters—one represents danger, and the other represents opportunity." What she—no—what both of us learned was that no opportunity for growth ever comes without risk. We can paralyze ourselves with fear in a crisis, or take it as an opportunity to be better than we think we are. Indeed, that is exactly what that young lady did. Her quiet power and dignity under pressure was humbling to me. I don't think I possess the words to describe how I felt, but what follows is a copy of the note I sent to her after the performance:

> I write to tell you how proud I was of you at last week's performance. When you sounded "that spot" in "that piece" and it sailed out with the tenderness, grace and reverence of the most seasoned professional, I smiled from ear to ear. Why? Not just because it was so incredibly beautiful, or that it is great when something that hard is played so well, but because I knew at

that moment you won. There is nothing harder in this world than beating self-doubt. And that, Nancy, is exactly what you did. I write to let you know how happy I was, and more importantly, how proud I was of you. It was a joy to behold. I hope you enjoy every moment of thinking about how incredibly you played. Now and in the future, you will always know *you won*.

I hope my students, and I, can *always* remember that everything worthwhile comes with some risk, and with every crisis comes a choice: we can view it as a problem or as an opportunity. As a ship in harbor is always safe, so are we when we turn our backs on a challenge which offers growth. However, just as that is not what ships are for, that is not what students—or their teachers—are for.

Nancy was a very special person. She never really stopped believing in herself. She just needed a tugboat to help guide her out of the harbor. ◼

"Getting Back On the Horse and Riding Even Harder"

Some years ago while at a convention, I was sitting in the audience for a performance by a very fine high school band. I was having a wonderful time enjoying the warmth of sound, sincerity of expression and quality of execution. As I listened, I could only think about how lucky those young people were to have that experience, and how lucky the audience was to witness their music making.

After a short time, I happened to notice that the person sitting next to me, a band director I knew, was writing in the margin of his program. I assumed he was making note of things he liked or questions he had about the work. But I realized the "notes" were only tick marks, like those used to keep score in a game. Curiosity getting the better of me, I asked him about those marks during a break between compositions. He told me he was "counting mistakes." I said, "What?" He repeated, "I'm counting mistakes."

Now as shocked as I was puzzled, I watched as I listened, and sure enough every time the band made any sort of error he put pen to paper for a hash mark. I couldn't stop watching him. I thought it was the most twisted thing I had ever seen. But it did start me thinking.

We music teachers spend a lot of time on mistakes. We guard against them, correct them, teach to prevent them, do exercises to cure them and listen for them intently. You may say we are somewhat preoccupied with them. They are a fact of our professional lives. Some, like the person described above, use them as a measuring stick; however, I think most of us use them simply to identify areas for further work.

But I fear our constant attention to errors in rehearsals can lead our students to measuring the success of their performance by the number of mistakes made. That has always concerned me. We certainly don't teach that view, but our constant work to remove errors and to give attention to them can lead our students to that conclusion. How can we help it? Here are a few thoughts.

Listen for Chills Not Spills

Every time I have students start to lament to me the mistakes they made in a performance, I stop them dead in their tracks and ask them to count the number of correct notes they played, and then come talk to me. I ask them to number the chills, the tingles up the spine, the tears, the goose bumps and the smiles of joy they had in a performance rather than the mechanical errors. Computers don't make mistakes, but they also can't express emotions.

You Can't Keep Going to the Edge and Not Fall Once in a While

They must learn that having ever-higher expectations, pushing themselves further and further to the edge is a good thing. But it has the inherent risk of error. Nonetheless, they need to know it is far better to try that hard and have the occasional fault, than to play it safe, maybe with fewer errors, and never reach for the stars. I like to think of those kinds of errors as "proactive mistakes." They are the ones we make in a sincere effort to try ever harder for ever better. I contrast those to "inactive mistakes."

Inactive mistakes are those made when we "zone out," disengage from rehearsals or simply stop trying as hard as we can. When Steve tries to play a passage softer than he ever has, and the sound gasps, that is a proactive mistake. When Bill simply forgets to come in, because he was thinking about lunch, that is an inactive mistake.

Keep it in Perspective

I tell my students that concerts don't matter to me, and I really don't care much about them. For me, they are a very insignificant activity. I do hope they go well so the students have a good experience, and their families and friends see the fruits of their efforts. But the truth is that I really don't care! Why? I go on to tell them I believe rehearsals are what matter. That is where the learning happens, that is where we *all* grow as people and as musicians, and come together to express our collective selves. Rehearsals are where we test our limits and reach for the unreachable. Rehearsals are where we play when no one is listening but *ourselves*.

I want them to feel good about themselves, their hard work, their progress and their successes based on *rehearsals*, not the one-time-through at a concert. Concerts have too many variables, not the least of which is nerves!

I explain, over and over, that the dress rehearsal is my favorite part of the process. To me it is the chance to "perform" for the right reasons. Not for applause, not for the audience, not for praise, just for each of us and the music.

"The Diet Syndrome"

I am the world's most experienced dieter. I hate them, but I am always on one. Here is how it usually goes: I start off the morning terrifically, with total control. I am a walking advertisement for willpower. At some point later in the day, I think, "Well, I have been so good, I'll just have one little piece of something naughty. What could that hurt?" At that very moment, my brain says, "That's it; the diet is shot, so I might as well eat two whole bags of Oreo cookies and a gallon of butter-pecan ice cream. Why not, my diet is ruined." You're wondering what that could possibly have to do with making mistakes. I think it has everything to do with it. So much so that before concerts I describe my dieting experience to every ensemble.

I tell them that someone will make a mistake during the concert. It may be me, it may be them or it may be all of us. We may even crash and burn, the piece completely falling apart. The trick is to go on after those mistakes, performing *even better*. I believe students frequently start a piece with the same control and enthusiasm as I start my diet. Then comes that first mistake in the piece and all too often they think, "That's it, this piece is ruined. So let's get it over with and go on to the next one."

At best, that attitude lessens the quality of the experience for the students and makes them feel as if they didn't succeed. At worst, it sets in motion a "why bother to concentrate now" sentiment that can result in a chain reaction of mistakes that can be technically catastrophic, let alone prevent a wonderful musical experience.

I then tell them a story. I once attended a concert by one of our country's premiere service bands. After a rousing opener, the band began a slow, lyrical piece playable by most any junior high school band. It was so nice to hear it performed in the hands of those master musicians. Then, on beat three of measure nine, when the horns were to come in on a unison half note in their most comfortable range, what was heard was the biggest crack you could imagine. Somehow, five horns entered with six cracks on that note. It was like someone had put a hand grenade in the horn section for that one pitch. For an average ensemble that wouldn't have been that big a deal, but for them it was. I go on to tell them the purpose of my story.

The fact that even players of that amazing caliber can make mistakes is important for every student to know, but it was what happened *after* the crack that mattered. It was astounding. Like me on my diet, they certainly could have collectively thought, "Well this piece is ruined, let's get on to the next one so we can show our true abilities." They didn't. As a matter of fact, nothing could be further from the truth. At that very moment, I saw all sixty players instantly come even farther to the edges of their chairs, sit up even straighter and glue their eyes on their conductor with a focus and concentration the likes of which I have never seen before. I am convinced that they didn't even blink their eyes for the next two hours. They simply decided they were not going to allow another error, in that piece, or any other. Truly, the rest of the performance was flawless and stunning, but the most wonderful part of the concert was seeing the ensemble rise to heights I have rarely heard as a result of that boo-boo.

I go on to say that we all "fall off the horse" sometimes, especially if we are riding as hard as we can. The trick is not just getting back on, but getting back on the horse and riding even harder. After an error, our students can throw their hands in the air in resignation, or they can use that "fall" as motivation. They can be encouraged to think to themselves, "Well, that mistake let everyone know we're human, now let's use every ounce of energy and concentration we have to make music with so much passion and intensity that we *prove* it!"

We can help students learn that incredibly valuable life lesson, best summed up in the words of Jalaluddin Rumi as quoted by Wayne Dyer: "The falls of our life provide us with the energy to propel ourselves to a higher level." If *all* we do is help those entrusted to us learn that simple truth, we will have succeeded. Everyone falls off a horse. Many can get back on. But extraordinary are those who can get back on and ride even harder. ▩

FAILURE IS OPPORTUNITY TURNED UPSIDE-DOWN

One evening, while conducting in Richmond, Virginia, I was driving with several teachers on our way to dinner. We were trying to find a restaurant in a congested part of town. As we got close to the restaurant, one gentleman said, "It's your next left turn." There was only one problem: a sign that said, "No Left Turn." The car filled with some tension as it seemed the sign would make our route to the restaurant impossible. At that moment, one teacher said, "Well, as one of my grade school teachers always said, 'Two wrongs don't make a right, but three rights make a left.'"

Not being the sharpest knife in the drawer, I sat there puzzled as I processed his words, drawing a sketch in my mind. And sure enough, he was *right*, well, correct. Three rights do make a left. What a perfect metaphor for failure. On the surface, we failed at making our needed left turn. However, our driver used that *opportunity* to *succeed* in putting us on a different path. One, I might add, that gave me the chance to see even more of the landmarks of that beautiful city. He didn't think he had failed, he didn't give up, he didn't panic. He saw that sign as a result, not a failure. He saw possibility and opportunity in finding a different way to achieve our goal.

Those words brilliantly describe how each of us, and our students, have choices every time we encounter what might be seen as failure.

What is Failure?

Truly, failure is a state of mind. It is all in how we see each of our attempts at something. Is each of them a negative event we dread, or is it just an outcome? As Wayne Dyer wrote, "You can never fail, you just produce results." How much easier it is for us to handle times when things don't happen the way we wish, when we view them simply as the result of what we did.

Give Yourself Permission to Fail

How many times have we been stopped by fear of failing? That fear can be powerful. And I think the younger the person the worse that fear is perceived. The first step in changing our students' attitudes about failure is simply convincing them it is okay to fail, that failing is simply one *possible* result of trying, but undoubtedly a *necessary* step in succeeding. As Marva Collins said, "If you can't make a mistake, you can't make anything." In the words of my dear friend Tim Lautzenheiser, "A mistake is at least evidence that someone tried to do something."

One of the greatest sentiments about giving oneself permission to fail comes from Samuel Beckett: "Ever tried. Ever failed. No matter. Try again. Fail again. Fail better." What a remarkable concept: *failing better*. How free is one who not only can embrace failure as *necessary*, but has given oneself permission not just to fail, but to fail better the next time?

Failure is Knowledge

Oscar Wilde said, "Experience is the name everyone gives to their mistakes." Those results we call failures are actually great sources of important data. With a healthy dose of reflection, each time we "fail" we become armed with valuable information that will make our next attempt more informed. Basically, failure is knowledge and knowledge is power. As Thomas Edison so eloquently stated, "I have not failed. I've just found 10,000 ways that won't work."

Every Failure is an Opportunity

I know it seems like optimism gone wild, but it's true. Each time we fail we are given a chance, a chance to try again, now far more knowledgeable about what works and what doesn't work. As Henry Ford perfectly concluded, "Failure is the opportunity to begin again, more intelligently."

Failure Might Require Change

Often we need only to be receptive to the thought that failure might require change and to be willing to look at the task at hand with different eyes. In that way, we will heed the warning of Helen Keller: "When one door of happiness closes, another opens; but often we look so long at the closed door that we do not see the one which has been opened for us." Focusing over and over on the same approach for the same goal may just make us spin our wheels

with great effort yet little reward. More often than not it is simply
having the ability to "Follow success with success; follow failure
with change."

Failure as a Challenge

Let's say we have achieved a specific goal and are now able to do
what we set out to accomplish. We succeeded. But what happens
when we try that same ability in a more difficult setting—raising the bar, if you will—and we fail. That failure has given us the
chance to become better at what we do by challenging our abilities. Doing a task or technique is good. Doing that same thing in a
more demanding situation is better. Remember the wonderful Af-
rican proverb that reminds us, "Smooth seas do not make skillful
sailors." Once we learn to sail, we only get better by challenging
ourselves with ever more choppy seas.

Failure Can Be Success

The remarkable Heraclitus offered this wisdom: "When there is
no sun, we can see the evening stars." Every time I think of that
statement I get chills. It is as true as it is powerful. Our goal may
be to see the beautiful mountains or breathtaking flowers of life. A
terrific goal. But if the sun goes down, leaving us in darkness, we
will fail. Often we will then expend enormous amounts of energy
bemoaning the darkness and cursing our failure. However, it is only
that darkness—the darkness that made us fail—that can offer us the
beauty of the night sky.

If we had spent all of our efforts trying to change or "fix" the
darkness, we would never have had the opportunity to see the majesty of the evening stars. True, we might just stumble upon those

moments by accident, but an open mind and a willingness to look beyond and around the failure may yield growth and beauty more magnificent than we ever imagined. Failure is many things, *not* all of which are bad; in fact, viewed correctly, failure can be a gift in disguise.

Failure is a Choice

Every time we don't succeed, or hit that "No Left Turn" sign, each of us—and each of our students—is faced with a decision. Do we give up or do we persevere? When we try to do something new or more difficult we often just can't make that "left turn." But is that a reason to give up? No; we might just have to change those "left turns" we want to make in life into "three right turns" in order to get where we want to go. Remember, "No one is a failure who keeps trying."

It is sad to come to understand that "Many of life's failures," as Thomas Edison reminds us, "are experienced by people who did not realize how close they were to success when they gave up." Those people simply didn't keep in mind those four Latin words which remind us: *Nemo nisi intus superatus.* ("You only get beaten from within.")

We can help our students to view failure as an outcome rather than a bad event, as an opportunity to find another way, as a chance to grow and learn, and to think around obstacles or failures. But of greater importance, we must teach them never to give up. Our students must come to learn, as the following anonymous poem asserts, the only thing which can stop them—is them. So maybe failure is quite simply opportunity turned upside down.

Don't Quit

When things go wrong as they sometimes will;
When the road you're trudging seems all uphill;
When the funds are low, and the debts are high
And you want to smile but have to sigh;
When care is pressing you down a bit—
Rest if you must, but do not quit.

Success is failure turned inside out;
The silver tint of the clouds of doubt;
And you can never tell how close you are
It may be near when it seems so far;
So stick to the fight when you're hardest hit—
It's when things go wrong that you must not quit.

"TOUCH THE WALL"

Try this: at your next rehearsal, have your ensemble hold a chord. Then stop them with a beautiful release. Next, ask them to repeat the chord, as softly as they can. Then, as they are holding that sound, vehemently tell them to get softer. They will; they always do!

Human nature being what it is, with all of us wanting to exert as little energy as possible, the reality of their "as soft as possible" was probably *comfortably* soft. I take that opportunity to tell them they lied to me! And that a lie is no way to further our relationship. "I *said*, 'Play it as softly as you can.' You played it softly. I said, 'Play it softer.' and you *did*. That is a lie! You obviously could play it softer; you just didn't want to go all the way to the wall."

I go on to point to a wall across the room, and tell them that our goal is to get all the way to that wall, and touch it. Each of *us* has to progress individually and collectively, and try as hard as we can to get there, pushing ourselves beyond what is comfortable. That every day we all need to move toward the wall, simply lessening the distance bit by bit.

Comfortable is a Habit

"Comfortable" becomes a habit because of familiarity and relative ease. The narrow range of what we can do with little effort becomes our everyday norm. Most of the difficulty in getting our students to work harder, and for our demanding more than we thought possible, is breaking the habit of working at an "acceptable" level. "The chains of habit are too weak to be felt," Samuel Johnson stated, "until they are too strong to be broken." We all know they *can* be broken; it's just that much harder to do.

However, on the positive side, just as working at a "comfortable" level can become habit, so too can always striving for better. If we train our students—and expect from ourselves—nothing but the best, that will become the new "normal." Aristotle made it so abundantly clear: "We are what we repeatedly do. Excellence, then, is not an act, but a habit."

Personal Responsibility

A key component of getting to that point is helping our students learn personal responsibility. They must come to realize that though the teacher is responsible for many aspects of the rehearsal, they too are responsible for much of what goes on. They are personally responsible for their posture, playing position, breath support, tone, intonation and instrument condition (whether that is their voice or something they put in a case). It is up to them to have pencils, mark their parts, stay focused, concentrate, watch the conductor and prepare for rehearsal by having practiced the work at hand in advance.

Not only do we need to convince every student of those responsibilities, we must get each of them to believe he or she is the *single most important person* in the room. We all have those students who come to us already self-motivated. They not only understand that responsibility, they live it every moment they are with us. But we also have those who have convinced themselves they don't matter. They think to themselves, "I'm not important so why work that hard?" That is as misguidedly wrong as it is patently sad.

Those students need to know their ensemble is like a chain made of individual people, no chain being stronger than its weakest link. There can be *no* weak link in a strong chain. The *strongest links* don't determine the strength of a chain, the *weakest* do. Strong links don't "balance out" weak ones. No ensemble's tone, intonation, phrasing, dynamics or anything else can be better than its weakest link. Period.

Another analogy I use with ensembles is that of their comprising a wonderful beef stew: "If I take a large pot and fill it with the finest pieces of beef money can buy, would you want to eat the beef stew?" They always answer "yes." "Now, if I add the finest carrots, would you still want to eat that beef stew?" Again, they answer "yes." "Then, if I add the best potatoes and onions to the pot, would you want to eat that beef stew?" At this point, especially if you use this analogy just before lunch, they adamantly say "yes."

"Now," I go on to ask, "if I add just one cockroach to the stew, would you still want to eat it?" Their answer of "no" is usually accompanied by raucous, nauseated gasps of sound. "That's right; no one would want to eat that stew. Even though every ingredient, shy one, was the finest possible, that one cockroach ruined the stew."

I always end the story with a simple statement: "Don't be the cockroach in the musical stew that is all of us. You must take personal responsibility to ensure the ingredient that is *you* is the finest possible—always. Because that ingredient is *the* most important one in the pot."

We Must Point the Way

Goals, especially lofty ones, can sometimes seem invisible. When the place someone seeks is miles down the road, it is out of sight. The best we as teachers can do is point in that direction, offer lots of encouragement, and make certain we praise the little steps along the way to the goal. In addition, however, *we* must set expectations, because students often don't know what to expect of themselves. High expectations are the goals *we are always pointing toward*—that place down the road, out of sight.

But as the Chinese proverb states, "You point your finger at the moon, the fool stares at your finger." We *must* point to the goal for our students, the goal of their each "reaching the moon," all the while making certain they truly understand that what we are asking them to "look at," or strive for, goes far beyond the obvious, everyday, going-through-the-motions of "getting through the music." *Getting through the music* which can be thought of as them simply staring at our finger.

Will some who watch us "point to the moon," "point to a wall," or "point to the stars," lack the optimism to look beyond our finger? Without a doubt. The trick is simply not letting them get in your way, or your students' way. As those naysayers stand there staring at your finger, make certain they are not blocking the view of the moon your students seek to see.

We Must Show Them the Way

Without question, we need to "show them the way" by teaching them what they need to know to improve and by creating an environment that is conducive to learning and growth. However, equally important—if not more important—is that we "show them the way" by our example. How better for them to learn the way of striving for excellence, hard work, always demanding more from themselves and personal responsibility, than from their modeling us?

Can it be frightening to put ourselves on the line like that? Yes, but as Sheldon Kopp put it so perfectly, "In the long run, we get no more than we have been willing to risk giving." Our students need to learn that lesson, but we must also know its truth for *ourselves*: we can expect no more from our students than we have been willing to risk showing them. Whether in preparation for rehearsal, practice for technical improvement or showing of passion in performance, we get what we are willing to model; rarely less and never more.

You Can Never Touch the Wall

It is said that "Good is not good enough if better is possible." Every day, progress must be made toward our goal of touching that wall. Each moment, trying harder to achieve or grow more. Each moment remembering the wisdom of Confucius: "It does not matter how slowly you go as long as you do not stop."

But what does that goal actually represent? Is it musical literacy, technical ability or creative thought? Yes, but it is using them to serve higher goals for our students: finding happiness; developing emotionally; expressing themselves; and communicating deeply, by making music more beautifully than they ever imagined. A monkey can "play" the notes. We must push our students to breathe life into those notes. And the wonderful thing about that goal: it lasts a lifetime. A quest with no end.

When I point to that wall, I ask my students to work to shorten the distance from "where we are" to the wall. And as we get closer, I ask them to strive for simply *cutting that distance in half*, over and over again, until they reach the wall. In that way, bit by bit, getting closer to the goal by constantly growing. Always demanding more of themselves, trying harder to reach *any* objective they set for themselves. That is by any standard a lofty goal, but what a wonderful one for them to learn and carry with them as they go through life.

However, there is a *far greater* lesson to be learned from that wall: no matter how hard you try, no matter how many times you simply cut the distance to any goal by half, "You can never touch that wall." This notion is an illustration of what is known as "Zeno's Paradox," put forward by the remarkable fifth-century thinker Zeno of Elea. He believed that continually halving the distance from one point to another brought to bear an answer represented by *infinity*.

Doesn't that theory represent our task in so many things in life? In music, no matter how far we travel toward the goal of musical expression, we can always go further. We can get close to the wall, but we can *never* touch it. It is always just out of reach, with infinite possibilities for continued growth.

Can that be a source of great frustration? Of course it can be, but when understood, it can also be exhilarating. There is always a higher mountain to climb, another journey to travel, another moon to point toward. I guess it all boils down to our getting every child to really understand—and hope we can get them to live their lives knowing—that "When you compete against others you strive for success. When you compete against yourself, you strive for excellence."

At your next rehearsal, when you ask your students for something, don't let them lie to you, don't let them lie to the music, don't let them lie to themselves. Point the way. Show the way. Help them to make a chain of habit called "always striving for excellence" that will touch every aspect of their lives. Go ahead, point to the moon. With your encouragement, they may just look right past that moon and be staring at the stars even farther away.

"WITHOUT YOU, THERE NEVER WOULD HAVE BEEN A JOURNEY."

Many years ago I was sitting at the desk in my office. I was tired and a bit frustrated. I had lost a few then-recent battles, wasn't really sure I was getting my message across to my students and had begun to feel more and more gloomy. As my son Matthew once profoundly philosophized at the ripe old age of nine, "I had too much on my plate, and was too tired to chew."

As I sat there staring at the wall in front of my desk, a student walked by my open door, peered in and saw me looking less than zippy. She said hello and asked if I was okay. In that I responded with a pretty dull, "sure," she perceptively said I looked tired and low and asked me what was wrong.

Her next words, however, shook me to the core, when she asked, "Has your star burned out?" I puzzled for a moment, then asked her what she meant. She went on to describe how my sparkle seemed faded. At that moment, *I* was as dumbstruck as *she* was correct. After she left, I couldn't stop thinking about what she had said. I couldn't stop thinking of how right she was. My star *had* certainly become dull.

A few days later, she came back to see me. She was carrying a box and an envelope, which she quietly presented to me. Her only instructions were to read the letter before opening the box. And oh what a letter it was. In it she described her journey as a student, and thanked me for being a part of that path. Through her words I realized, more than ever before, how important the glow of our excitement and enthusiasm can be to our students. And that we can never allow anything to stand in the way of it shining light on the path that is the journey of learning. She ended her letter—this magnificent letter—with nine words I will never forget, nine words that centered my focus, nine words that strengthened my resolve, nine words I will spend the rest of my life trying to deserve. "Just remember," she wrote, "without you, there never would have been a journey."

Utterly speechless, almost trembling at the thought of what she had written, I opened the box. There I saw a beautiful, shining, silver paperweight in the shape of a perfect five-point star. On it were engraved those nine amazing words. Those nine words that took my breath away.

The problem was that I forgot. I forgot how important what we do, how we do it, and who we are, can be. I forgot sometimes we lose those battles but win a much more important war. I forgot the insight of Cullen Hightower who declared, "A true measure of your worth includes all the benefits others have gained from your success." I forgot the wisdom of Benjamin Disraeli who proclaimed, "The greatest good you can do for another is not just to share your riches but to reveal to him his own." I forgot the perceptiveness of Sir Winston Churchill who affirmed, "We make a living by what we get, we make a life by what we give." I forgot the brilliance of Galileo who advised, "You cannot teach a man anything, you can only help him discover it within himself."

I forgot my purpose—my *true* purpose—best described in the wonderful Irish proverb: "The tree remains, but not the hand that planted it."

I forgot. I simply forgot. But all at once, holding that star, the shining light of that student—that extraordinary student—helped me to remember the joy of teaching, the impact of teaching and the responsibility of teaching. She reminded me of the profound honor it is to help young people discover that learning is not a destination, but a journey, an incredibly wonderful journey to be devoured, savored and cherished. More significantly, she reminded me of just how lucky we are to get to share that journey with all whom we teach.

Are there still those days I can feel my star fading? Absolutely. But then I look at my paperweight star and remember. I remember the remarkable kindness of an equally remarkable student. I remember the faces of those I have had the privilege to teach. I remember their smiles, their tears, their frustrations, their successes. But mostly I remember the importance, the incredible importance of what we do.

So the next time you feel your star begin to fade, look deeper into your students' eyes and remember those words—those nine simple words. Remember your purpose. Remember *what you are* in the lives of your students. Remember their faces. But above all else, remember that "Without *you*, there never would have been a journey." A precious journey indeed. Remember. ▦

WHY DIDN'T *I* THINK OF THAT?

There I was in the middle of rehearsing the University Symphonic Band. Though most of the piece was being played extremely well, there was one section of the composition that was going to be my undoing. It was a very long passage of rapid double-tonguing for the entire trumpet section. It seemed to go on for months. The fatigue factor was great to say the least. With that in mind, I asked the trumpets to platoon the part, taking turns with each playing a few measures at a time.

Normally, that would have solved the problem, but it didn't. It was okay at best. Running pitches, passed between parts, added a measure of difficulty I hadn't foreseen. So I explained the problem and offered a solution. We tried it. It failed. I tried another solution. It failed. And another and another and another. They all failed to make it significantly better, bogging down the rehearsal and our collective spirit. Talk about fatigue! I gave up and moved on.

From then until the next rehearsal, I thought of little more than that passage, racking my brain for a way to help the now-frustrated trumpet players. The rehearsal came, I explained my solution, we tried it and it promptly ended in disaster. I think it may have made matters worse. So I dropped it immediately and moved on. Again, after that rehearsal I tried to find an answer. I became obsessed with finding a solution. Finally I thought of a good one, or so I thought.

The next rehearsal, my "new" solution failed more miserably than all the others put together. Finally, I looked at the trumpeters, gave a giant sigh of disappointment and said, "I just don't know what to do." At that very moment, one of my bass clarinetists said, "Why don't you try...," whereupon he described his suggestion. It was perfect. At once we *all* knew *that* was the solution. He found the best answer to the puzzle.

It was one of the happiest moments in my entire teaching career. Sure I had been wrong a zillion times before and had gone back to the drawing board just as often. And yes, students had often figured out ways to improve our performance far better than I had. But there was something special about that day. It represented a sort of climax of all those moments. I was overcome by a feeling of accomplishment and pride. Why? Because for me, it represented a peak experience. It was a most tangible moment of success. I really felt like I had made it: my students were so much smarter than me! The obsolescence—knowledge that I was unnecessary—I had dreamed of was really at hand.

I felt pretty darned proud. Not only did a student figure it out, but here was a bass clarinetist, whose part didn't contain that passage at anytime in the piece, so engaged in rehearsal that he attended to the trumpet players' plight. This wasn't just your everyday garden-variety "my students knew better than I did." This was the "Grand Poobah" of "I tried again and again, I thought it over and over, I gave it my best and they still figured it out better." I was the happiest teacher on the planet!

Richard Bach wrote, "Learning is finding out what you already know. Doing is demonstrating that you know it. Teaching is reminding others that they know it just as well as you." And I hope you will agree the proof of *really* teaching is when they know it better than we do. For what is our true goal? To make them *know* or to make them *think*? As Socrates stated, "I cannot teach anybody anything. I can only make them think."

I recently had a rehearsal with my Wind Ensemble back at the university. In the middle of rehearsing a work, I pointed out what I thought was a moment of genius by the composer. The ensemble was unmoved. They sat there somewhat lifelessly. I went on about this and finally said, "Why is it that I'm the only one who thinks this is so amazing?" To which a clarinetist (you have to watch them, they're usually the quiet ones) chimed in, "Because you're crazy!" I loved it. It makes me happy that my students feel comfortable enough to laugh at me, challenge me and correct me. Does that often point out my limitations and weaknesses? Yes, but it also gives me an opportunity to model my favorite lesson: one must never stop learning, therein living the words of William Cowper, "Knowledge is proud that he has learn'd so much; Wisdom is humble that he knows no more."

I figure it this way: as long as I am prepared, working my hardest and showing I am always trying to learn more, every mistake I make is part of my teaching. Every blunder I make is a good thing, for if I share those mistakes with my students I save them the time, effort and energy of making the mistakes themselves. Like parents hope their children will do and have better than they did, every teacher hopes their students will learn and be even more than they are.

How wonderful is the class or rehearsal where the teacher fosters creative thinking, problem solving and coming up with better ways. How wonderful is it when the students become the teacher. How wonderful is it when we know we truly succeeded. Leonardo da Vinci affirmed, "Poor is the pupil who does not surpass his teacher." But if we help our students learn, and create an environment of creative challenge, then we can add to that great master's statement: *Truly rich are teachers whose students grow to surpass them.*

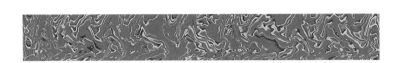

WORRY

I don't like to worry, though Lord knows I do more than my fair share of it. For certain aspects of my life I have elevated worrying to an art form. You might say that if worrying became an Olympic sport I would be a gold-medal winner with few contenders in my league. But as much as I worry about most everything in life, I almost never worry about rehearsals. Odd, isn't it? One would think those intense sessions would be the source of many worries, but strangely they are not. Why? It doesn't make any sense.

I don't know about you, but I worry about what I can't control: that for which I feel helpless. I believe that if we have prepared as much as we could, we shouldn't be worried. We have done all we could. It's when we haven't prepared as well as possible that worry has every right to take hold of us. If we walk into a rehearsal with a firm knowledge of our scores and a detailed lesson plan, what is there to worry *about*? We have done everything possible to ensure success. That is also a lesson I try to pass along to students. Whether one is studying for an exam or performing a solo, worrying is wasted energy. Preparation is proactive energy. Once we feel we have truly prepared to our best ability, worry has no purpose. I know it's easier said than done, but it is too logical to be

ignored. As my dear friend Jerry Tyson says, "Worry is only bor-
rowing from tomorrow's problems, bringing no relief from those
of today." How very true!

The remarkable Leo Buscaglia offered the same sentiment with,
"Worry never robs tomorrow of its sorrow, it only saps today of its
joy." But my favorite thought regarding the foolishness of spending today worrying about tomorrow was given to me by my then
seven-year-old son Matthew, quoting a "SpongeBob SquarePants"
cartoon in which Mr. Krabs ended an argument with the profound
words: "What is today but yesterday's tomorrow?" Just remember
that today is the tomorrow you worried about yesterday!

If we are ill-prepared, causing us to worry, we won't enjoy our
art, our students or the precious time we have to make music.
Worrying is no fun. It eats us alive, ages us and tends to make us
negative and surly. Worry predisposes us to being in a defensive,
survival mode rather than an optimistic, offensive posture. The
confidence fueled by preparation leads us to be receptive and eager about the road ahead rather than to be worried about what's
around the next turn. Our students will learn that valuable lesson
from our example. Worry on the face or in the voice of a conductor translates to fear and trepidation for ensemble members who
are looking to their conductor as a model. They may not even
know what to worry about, but worry they will if that's how we
condition them.

I don't like to worry and I don't like what my worrying does to
my students. Knowing I have done all I can before each rehearsal
prevents me from having to fret. That way I can save all that good
worrying for everything else in my everyday life. ∎

DON'T ALWAYS
THINK BIG

What we do can be overwhelming in so many ways. The myriad tasks and responsibilities we have every day can be exhausting. As can be the fact that what we do is never done: we are always taking our students to the next step. And once they get to that step, we are off to one even further away. Think of all we do: clerical duties, meetings, preparation, fundraising, concerts and the like. Also, adding to the frustration, by nature of what we do and probably how we were trained, we spend an enormous amount of time looking for errors.

We worry about fixing the chord that is out of tune and often miss the fact—and chance to celebrate—the rest of the piece is beautifully in tune. We agonize about Billy not being able to play over the break more than that he smiled in rehearsal when we told him he had great posture. We fret and beat ourselves up over the fact the band can't play grade three music for spring contest rather than take pride in the fact that two years before, grade three could just as well have been grade eighteen because all they could play then was grade one-half.

We are nitpickers, faultfinders, error-recognition machines, and that is often what we were taught to be. It's great at times, but it can be very overwhelming, frustrating and defeating. The trick is that when all looks so bad, we must *find* the positives. We must force ourselves to think of our successes. We must notice the small joys in our everyday activities.

Some years ago at a convention, a young lady came up to speak with me after a workshop I had given. She looked sad, tired and drained. She proceeded to tell me she was ready to leave the profession. I asked her to share her thoughts. She said she still loved music, children and teaching, but felt she made little difference. She truly felt as though she had accomplished nothing; she saw no progress in her students. We spent some time chatting. I asked her to describe any recent rehearsal. She did so sullenly. After each pessimistic statement she made about the rehearsal, I asked questions to guide her to "notice" little accomplishments, moments of real progress no matter how small.

With help, she found many such moments. The answer for her, and for so many of us, is to *think small*. While walking to the office, packing up the cart, or putting away materials after teaching a class, lesson or rehearsal, we must think of moments to be happy about, like photos for a scrapbook: tiny victories, a student's smile or a moment of success. We must savor those memories, no matter how small. With perspective, patience and perseverance as our guide, we must notice every little accomplishment.

No matter how we do it, we need to take stock of our "photos" and remember our impact. Impact which is sometimes difficult to measure and often comes in steps so small as to be *almost* imperceptible. In the words of the Nobel Prize winning chemist, Marie Curie, "One never notices what has been done; one can only see what remains to be done." The next time you're frustrated by thinking nothing positive has happened, pull out that scrapbook of memories; then smile. ▪

"WHEN YOU WISH UPON A STAR..."

O ptimist: a person with a positive attitude; someone who tends to take a hopeful and positive view of future outcomes; *see also teacher!*" Well, that last bit wasn't actually part of the definition of an optimist, but it should be. Let's face it; one can't dedicate one's life to teaching without being an optimist. We take those who don't know, and believe we can help them to learn. Who but an optimist could do that? It is part of what we are and what we do. It is education.

Now those who know me are reeling as they read this. Why? Because I am a card-carrying pessimist. In fact, I have elevated pessimism to an art form. My wife's favorite line to me is, "That's right, no matter how dark it gets, keep pulling the shades down." At the office, I am known as the department's resident pessimist. Yes, sadly, it's true.

I must share with you that as I am working on this chapter about being an optimist I am laughing out loud. Why? Because I'm writing it while sitting on an airplane at the end of a runway at LaGuardia Airport where I have been parked for over an hour, on my way out of town for a band festival. This, after having spent the previous seven hours waiting in the terminal.

Thinking optimistically is truly the farthest thing from my mind right now. Whether it's steaming about this flight or most anything else in life, I am a pessimist—about everything *except* teaching. I know it sounds odd, but it's the truth. Without a healthy dose of optimism we can't effectively teach. We must believe we can educate and inspire our students and that they can learn and flourish.

Hope

It isn't a case of seeing the glass half empty or half full. We must go even further and see the glass as *twice as big as it needs to be.* Always hopeful, even—or should I say especially—when our students or those around us don't see much reason to be hopeful. As the remarkable Christopher Reeve said, "There's no such thing as false hope—just hope."

Perfection

One must not let *the perfect* become the enemy of *the possible.* That may be one of the most important things we can teach our students. How often does a fear of not doing "it" *perfectly* stop us from trying at all? It's far easier to be a pessimist and say, "I won't be able to do it perfectly, so why try at all," than to try and see if it's possible. Our students need to learn from our example, and support, that perfection is unattainable for most things in life. Our striving for making something possible is virtually the only thing *that is* truly perfect!

Confidence

Our optimism can also help those entrusted to us to believe in themselves. What could be more optimistic? They need to learn that hoping and dreaming yields results when they *believe*. As the old expression goes, "Goals are simply dreams with deadlines." One evening at the dinner table my teenaged daughter, Meredith, summed it up better than I ever could, saying, "When you wish upon a star, you are really talking to yourself." To this day, I marvel at the profound power of those words. Wishes can come true with a heartfelt measure of optimism. But every teacher *knows* that. ▉

"Don't Hide Your Light Under a Bushel"

M usic teachers are an amazing lot. Our days are filled with so many tasks that we couldn't begin to list them in detail. Even if we could, why bother because no one would believe us? Between the amount of time teaching, planning and sequencing material, writing lesson plans, studying scores, corresponding with parents and administrators, not to mention fund-raising, instrument repair, hall duty, equipment maintenance, designing bulletin boards, recruiting, phone calls, paperwork, meetings, and the always-on-call "counseling" practice you make available to everyone in the band room, we have little time for the other 6,371 things we do every day.

We're constantly pulled in so many different directions. We are juggling so many balls in the air at one time, it is often hard to keep track of them, let alone juggle them. Though we often get tired (how's that for an understatement!) and sometimes get anxious (stop laughing and then read: crazed) we get it all done. My concern is all too often the casualty of this intensely demanding occupation is *us*.

Don't get me wrong. I'm not talking about the quality of our teaching or the talent for what we do. I am not speaking of our commitment, dedication or ability. I'm talking about how we are *perceived* by our students. Does our incredible workload manifest itself in a way that makes us come across to our students as angry, stressed, impatient, frustrated, short-tempered, unhappy or depressed?

We obviously love music and young people and are dedicated to the teaching of our art to those entrusted to us. We wouldn't still be teaching if we weren't. Quite simply, it's not our knowledge or ability that is diminished by this pace, it's our enthusiasm for what we do and for what our students are doing. We are often so drained by our responsibilities that something must give. We won't shirk any task because we are too dedicated; as a result, sometimes we just can't muster the energy to show our enthusiasm. But we must. At any cost, it must shine through to all.

In his book, *The Inner Game of Music*, Barry Green describes a performance he played under the baton of the remarkable Leonard Bernstein: "Bernstein's infectious enthusiasm (and unfocused eyes) convinced orchestral players and audience alike that they were witnessing some kind of privileged communication between Bernstein and Brahms. It's as though Bernstein somehow becomes the pure energy of the music he conducts. And his own sense of being caught up in the music communicates itself to his musicians, who find themselves also caught up in his inspiration and able to let go to his direction." We need always to strive to be that pure energy of the music, and we can't let anything stand in our way.

I hope you have read the incredible book *Tuesdays with Morrie*. It is a life-changing, life-affirming experience. In it Professor Morrie Swartz offers lessons on "life." Since reading that book, when confronted by a problem, I often wonder what advice Morrie would give me. What would Morrie say about the problem we just described? Some years ago, I was told he particularly liked an old proverb that offers the counsel, "Don't hide your light under a bushel."

But what is our light? Is it our knowledge? I don't think so. I am convinced our light is our enthusiasm. Our knowledge, talent and skill are *in us*, but that "light" of enthusiasm and excitement is necessary for all our students *to see it!* A porch light simply shows you where the door to a home is located so you know where to enter to find the joy of what's inside.

That light of our enthusiasm is what helps generate in our students a feeling of excitement for our art and for the process of learning that art. Our light of enthusiasm sets a positive mood in the classroom. It encourages our students to concentrate with intensity. Clearly, our students look toward us to be a source of knowledge, but, even more, they look toward us to be the source of energy and excitement for the journey to attain that knowledge. From that light they will come to realize how much we love our music and how excited we are to share it with them.

We can never underestimate what our enthusiasm does for our students. They may not know what reaching the goal will feel like. They may not understand all they will need to learn to get there. They may not even understand why they are going there at all. But they will sense, from our excitement for what we do, that it is worth the effort.

Will we continue to be stressed? Yes. Will we have those days where our battery is blinking the low-voltage warning light? You bet. Will the level of our enthusiasm and excitement always be vulnerable to the strains of our work? Absolutely. But the next time you walk into a rehearsal or class with the weight of our profession on your shoulders, or feel wiped out from fatigue, or have simply had a rotten day, before you allow anything to take its toll on your enthusiasm, think of Morrie. I guarantee if you have read the book or have seen the movie, you wouldn't—no, you couldn't—ever dream of letting yourself hide your light under a bushel.

Put simply, we must check our problems at the door as we walk into our rehearsals and classes. I know that's easier said than done, but what's at stake is far too important to settle for anything less. A few years ago I was given the following story. In its simplicity is profound advice.

The Small Tree

The plumber I hired to help me restore an old farmhouse had just finished a rough first day on the job. A flat tire made him lose an hour of work, his electric drill quit and now his ancient one ton truck refused to start. While I drove him home, he sat in stony silence. On arriving, he invited me in to meet his family. As we walked toward the front door, he paused briefly at a small tree, touching the tips of the branches with both hands.

When opening the door he underwent an amazing transformation. His tanned face was wreathed in smiles and he hugged his two small children and gave his wife a kiss. Afterward he walked me to the car. We passed the tree and my curiosity got the better of me. I asked him about what I had seen him do earlier.

"Oh, that's my trouble tree," he replied. "I know I can't help having troubles on the job, but one thing's for sure, those troubles don't belong in the house with my wife and the children. So I just hang them up on the tree every night when I come home and ask God to take care of them. Then in the morning, I pick them up again. Funny thing is," he smiled, "when I come out in the morning to pick 'em up, there aren't nearly as many as I remember hanging up the night before."

Every time I read that story I am reminded of how important it is for my "light" to shine every time I teach. My enthusiasm cannot be diminished by troubles, stress or fatigue. So, following the wisdom of that plumber, I use my office doorknob as my trouble tree. I know it seems ridiculous, but I do. Each time I close the door on my way to teach, I hold that handle for a brief moment and remember what is truly important. Then I am free to be the teacher I want to be. Yes, I am fully aware "reality" will be waiting for me when I pick up that "baggage" as I open my office door upon my return, but for that brief time I am free of anything that could drain my enthusiasm. Is it a bit silly? Yes, it probably is, but I know I am a better teacher because of it. Try it. It certainly is easier than planting a small tree in the hallway outside your classroom!

We know how important our enthusiasm is. It lights a path. And we know that path is too valuable, too precious, too profound, too fragile to risk any single student getting lost or falling without our light. That's just what we teachers do. Morrie knew. Boy, did he know. I wish for our profession, and for all those entrusted to it, that his wisdom will never be diminished by his passing. Let us all hope to have a light as brilliant and powerful as his, and allow no bushel ever to cause it harm.

WHY DO WE TEACH?

Have you ever asked yourself that question? More importantly, have you ever been able to answer it? If you are anything like me, your answer can be short and simple, or lofty and philosophical. It is, however, sometimes difficult to describe to others. When I think about that question, I always remember back to something Vaclav Nelhybel said to me many years ago while we worked together writing his biography. One day I asked him *why* he composed. His answer has stayed with me, echoing in my mind. In the most reverent tone he said, "Composing is the best means for me to manifest my existence as a human being...to communicate with those that I have never met, and those that I will never meet...giving me the satisfaction of knowing that I have spent my life meaningfully."

Isn't that why we teach music? You may agree with the first and last part of that quote, but wonder if the middle is relevant to teaching. That is the most important part of all. Think about it: when we teach young people the joys of music, they will support their children learning music, and their children's children. By helping our students to learn important lessons about hard work, teamwork, handling failure and believing in the power of their dreams, we encourage them to teach those lessons to their children, and they to their children. By helping those we teach become caring, sensitive, emotional people, they will pass those qualities along to generations we will never meet. In that way, we will change the lives of human beings farther than we see, and for longer than we can imagine.

We all know there will be frustrations, not the least of which is having students forget what we thought they learned. But the frustrations pale by comparison to the importance of our mission. My favorite story about "kids forgetting" was told to me by a middle school band director. His students were scheduled for a playing exam where they were to demonstrate their abilities on material recently learned. A young man was to have his exam on a Thursday. However, due to conflicts, he missed his allotted time. The teacher asked him to take the exam a few days later. During the test, the teacher asked the student to perform a chromatic scale. The student could not. The teacher then asked the boy why he had not learned the scale. The student's response was that he *had* learned it for last Thursday, but *hadn't* learned it for *today*.

That story got me thinking. How much material you once learned for an exam have you now forgotten? How would you fare on a test on the table of periodic elements, French verb tenses or algebraic formulas? If you are anything like me, that information, once known pretty well, is long gone. Was learning it useless? No, it had its purpose. The truth is our students may forget many things *we* teach them. But they will never forget the important things, because our final exam is ultimately: chills up the spine, a tingling feeling, tears, goose bumps, hair standing on end, and emotions coursing through every fiber of one's being.

That's why we teach. Because teaching *is* the best means for us to manifest our existence as human beings, to communicate with those we have never met, and those we will never meet, giving us the satisfaction of knowing we have spent our lives meaningfully. Rich is the man or woman who can look into the eyes of a child and see pride, satisfaction, a tear, a smile. What better way could there be to spend one's life? As Ken Hudgins states, "The meaning of life is to give life meaning." All teachers do just that for themselves, their students and for many who they will never know.

The answer to why we teach can be found in every educator's heart, but one day I found the answer on the floor. During a lunch break while visiting a high school to present a workshop, I was asked if I wanted a tour of their new building. Though still under construction, it was beautiful. My host and I walked the hallways admiring the quality of the workmanship and design. At one point, we were standing in what was to be the new lobby of the school. Embedded in the floor was a large replica of the school's seal. Looking down on that seal, I saw the words of the school's motto, written to inspire every student ever to enter the building. There I found the answer to why we teach: "Today we follow. Tomorrow we lead." And lead they will. How's that for summing up the influence of *every* teacher?

"Even a Fool Knows You Can't Touch the Stars..."

What a pessimistic title. But isn't that what we as teachers do? We try to get our students to "touch the stars" every moment of every waking day. So is that quest the ultimate in "tilting at windmills?" Is it foolish even to try? Well, that quote started me thinking, and I realized that being a music teacher *is just that*. We help young people reach for the stars. But according to that quote, it's futile. That led me to a very good question: what's at the core of people who would dedicate their lives to something that futile? Otherwise put, what is at the heart of being a music teacher? I really wanted to know for two reasons: to help me explain it to others, and more importantly, to remind myself of the teacher I want to be. Sadly, not the teacher I *am* every day, but the teacher I *want to be* every day.

In addition to being futile, isn't trying to touch the stars risky? You bet. But isn't there some risk in every worthwhile pursuit? Doesn't growth require us to take risks? And isn't that a lesson we want our students to learn? Janet Rand stated it so very eloquently: "The person who risks nothing, does nothing, has nothing, is nothing, and becomes nothing. He may avoid suffering and sorrow, but he simply cannot learn, feel, change, grow or love. Chained by his certitude, he is a slave; he has forfeited his freedom. Only the person who risks is truly free."

But what *is* the risk in trying to touch the stars? Fear we won't be able to reach them? Fear of looking silly for trying so hard? Fear of traveling unfamiliar paths? Fear of stepping into the unknown? Probably, a bit of all of those come into play. Maybe it's just a matter of remembering, as Patrick Overton wrote, "When you come to the edge of all the light you have, and must take a step into the darkness of the unknown, believe that one of two things will happen: either there will be something solid for you to stand on, or, you will be taught how to fly." Isn't that a wonderful sentiment? We often don't know when or where growth and learning will come to us. And we all know that some of the greatest accomplishments occur while we are trying to do something very different. So we don't end up touching the stars; settling for touching the moon isn't so bad.

Or is the fear merely a lack of confidence? Are we afraid to try simply because we doubt our abilities? Does our image of who and what we are—or, more disconcertingly, who and what we can become—prevent us from even trying to touch those stars? "It's not what you are that holds you back," warns Denis Waitley, "it's what you think you are not." Truer words may not exist.

I guess it doesn't matter whether it's a fear of failure, a fear of stepping outside comfort zones, or a lack of confidence. A big part of our job is convincing our students to reach, despite the fact that "Even a fool knows you can't touch the stars...." In thinking further, I realize we do that by *who* we teach, *what* we teach and *how* we teach.

Who We Teach

Who *do* we teach? Every student we see. From the cream of the crop—the best and the brightest—to those who struggle at every turn. It doesn't matter, we teach all of them. As Robert D. Ramsey observed, the magic of that is, "You have to stay ahead of the fastest pupil and remain right alongside the slowest pupil at the same time."

We see in them, every one of them, unlimited potential. We look at *every* student like a sculptor looks at a block of marble. We see in them what others, even they, can't see. It's like when the great Michelangelo created his magnificent statue of David, a statue he created from a single piece of marble—a piece of marble other sculptors looked at and refused to work on because it had an enormous flaw running through almost the entire slab. When he was asked how he did it, Michelangelo responded, "I saw the angel in the marble and carved until I set him free. David was always in the marble."

Simply put, we envision what our students can become and then we work to make it happen. We see what's possible, and then *teach* until we set them free to be what they can be. It is then they realize our goal: what once was *never imagined* possible, is *now* possible. It doesn't matter whether our students move in giant steps or baby steps, take to it naturally or with great effort. We take them from where they are—how they are—and gently help them try to touch the stars. Whenever I think of that, I am reminded of the wonderful story that follows. It is as poignant as it is appropriate to the question of *who* we teach.

The Pot That Was Cracked

An elderly Chinese woman had two large pots. Each hung on the ends of a pole which she carried across her shoulders. One of the pots had a crack in it, and at the end of the long walk from the stream to her house arrived only half full. The other pot, however, was perfect and always delivered its full measure of water.

For a full two years this went on daily, with the woman bringing home only one and a half pots of water. Of course, the perfect pot was proud of its accomplishments. But the poor cracked pot was ashamed of its own imperfection, and miserable that it could only do half of what it had been made to do.

After two years of what it perceived to be bitter failure, it spoke to the woman one day by the stream. 'I am ashamed of myself, because this crack in my side causes water to leak out all the way back to your house.' The old woman smiled, 'Did you notice that there are flowers on your side of the path, but not on the other pot's side? That's because I have always known about your flaw, so I planted flower seeds on your side of the path, and every day while we walk back, you water them. For two years I have been able to pick these beautiful flowers to decorate the table. So you see, without you being just the way you are, there would not be this beauty to grace the house.'

Each of us has our own unique flaws. But it's the cracks and flaws we each have that make our lives together so very interesting and rewarding. We just have to take every person as they are, and each of us remember to smell the flowers on our side of the path.

What We Teach

What *do* we teach? Well, Gustav Mahler said it perfectly: "What is best in music is not to be found in the notes." Yes we teach music, but that is simply a vehicle for so much more. We give our students a window to their souls. We teach them how to express themselves emotionally. We allow them to grow and develop as feeling, caring people, and in so doing help mold the future for generations we will never see.

We help young people understand why Mahler also stated, "If a composer could say what he had to say in words he would not bother trying to say it in music." In that way, living the words of Khalil Gibran: "O music, in your depths we deposit our hearts and souls. Thou hast taught us to see with our ears and hear with our hearts."

That's why trying to enumerate all that we teach is so difficult. But in that frustration I am reminded of the incredible words of Albert Einstein: "Not everything that can be counted counts and not everything that counts can be counted."

How We Teach

The obvious answer is that we use techniques, methods, codified approaches, and the resources of years of training. But that is only the tip of the iceberg. How do we *really* teach? To me, the answer comes from the words of Edith Wharton, who stated, "There are two ways of spreading light: to be the candle or the mirror that reflects it."

We can be the candle, training and teaching our students facts, concepts, knowledge and techniques. But more importantly, far more importantly, we can be the mirror, helping them see their accomplishments, the beauty they create and the miracle they are. We want students to appreciate themselves, enjoy hard work, treasure every moment of their lives, learn to give of themselves, learn to invest in themselves and savor the world. We each do that by being a mirror, reflecting back upon our students, simply showing them what had been there all along: themselves.

With all that said, I have come to know that "what's at the heart of being a music teacher" *is* the essence of the simple quote I started this chapter with: "Even a fool knows you can't touch the stars...." However, I guess I should tell you *the rest* of the quote. It comes to us from Judge Harry T. Stone, the remarkable character played by Harry Anderson on the television show "Night Court," in which the venerable jurist so eloquently stated, "Even a fool knows you can't touch the stars, but it doesn't stop a wise man from trying." But you already knew that, because that's what every music teacher knows, believes and lives. Whether our students ever get close to a star or not, they will be all the better for having tried.

THE LIST

Have I mentioned how much I appreciate your sharing time with me? And I hope our paths cross soon. It will be wonderful to see you *again*. That's right, "again." You may not remember, but we went to school together. You remember me, don't you? Surely you do! We were in the same ensemble back in school. Remember? I sat in the back row with the trumpets, so you might not remember *me*, but how could anyone forget that amazing person who taught us? That special, incredible teacher who made all the difference in the world. Of course you remember who I mean! Can't you just picture her face?

I remember how much she loved music. How much she cared about us. How much our success mattered. More significantly, how much we mattered as people. She never crossed the line of demanding too much, but never let us settle for too little. She was the very embodiment of kindness, support, dedication, perseverance, humility, concern, pride, warmth, artistry, zeal and passion. She gave freely of her wisdom, heart and soul. No matter how angry she may have ever been with us as performers, she was never angry with us as human beings. She cared as much about her art as she did about her students. She was as concerned about our growth as musicians as she was with our growth as people.

She was always there with that friendly smile, that knowing grin, and that raised-eyebrow look of worry. She always knew when we goofed, but never made us feel bad. She reveled in our every success. We could go to her with any problem. We could always trust her advice. We could always look to her as a model musician, teacher and person. Can't you remember thinking you wanted to be just like her? I know I did. Wow, I miss her so much.

I hope by now you are saying to yourself: "Maybe he *was* there. Did he have *my* teacher too?" Well, I know her because I had the "same teacher." Mine just happened to be in a small town in Pennsylvania! Indeed, I would venture to say that we all had *that* special music teacher, somewhere, at some time. And if we were very, very lucky, we had several of them.

Can't you just picture that teacher? I bet you often find yourself saying: "What would he have done in this situation?" or "How did she do that?" But have you ever stopped to think about what attributes made that person so special? What made him or her different from most every other teacher you had?

A few years ago at the dinner table with my family, we had a discussion about teachers. At the ripe old ages of fourteen, twelve and eight, my children thought they had the perspective to compare all of their previous teachers. The conversation then turned to the teachers my wife and I had at their ages. It got me thinking. Starting with kindergarten and moving forward, I tried to remember each of my teachers, in every subject. I found it interesting that for some of them I could remember their maiden and their married names, but for others I couldn't remember anything. Why? Why do I remember Miss Clark (who became Mrs. Paul midyear) from kindergarten, but can't remember any of my high school English teachers? I always thought fondly of my favorite teachers, but I never sat down to wonder why. What made them amazing, and impossible to forget?

Though this may seem like a stroll down "memory lane," I believe it can be far more than simply reminiscing. It is teacher-training at its best. If we take stock of the qualities of those we found to be remarkable teachers, and look for commonalities, we can make certain to embody those very qualities. If we take the best attributes from our very best teachers, we will ensure our success, and more importantly, the success of our students. How did that incredible math teacher handle discipline problems? How did that wise French teacher balance expectations with reality so well? What was it about that choir director's pacing that made it amazing? What trick did that science teacher use to get us to remember things? What was it about the way that band director gave directions that made it so easy to understand everything?

Remember those wonderful words of George Santayana, "Those who cannot remember the past are condemned to repeat it." I believe it is equally true that those who remember the best of the past *can* repeat it. We must learn from others' mistakes and failings, just as we learn from our own mistakes and failings. However, we must take the time to remember the wonder of our past teachers' excellence and repeat that, just as we repeat our own excellent moments as teachers. We can never forget that those faces staring back at us *now* will someday sit at the kitchen table with their children and recall all of *their* amazing teachers. Every day, we must do our best to make certain we are on *their lists*.

As to my list, Mr. Peiffer, my high school band director, would certainly be near the top. I am sure you had a Mr. Peiffer. I would watch him conduct a band rehearsal and think: "That is *what* I want to be." Little did I know what I really meant was, "That is *who* I want to be." I didn't know if he was the finest band director on the planet or the best teacher who ever held a baton. It certainly wasn't that we always saw eye to eye. But he was incredible in so many ways. He was always the teacher, always prepared and eager, always a gentleman, always the mentor, always the cheerleader, always the role model. He never let us give up on ourselves. He never let us settle for less than our best. He always praised the little steps along the way. He was always dedicated, fair, honest and encouraging. He truly loved music and shared that love with all those he taught. He was always ready to give an extra lesson, or play duets, or explain the next step along the way. He meant the world to me.

I remember one day in particular. Back in high school, two of us were chosen to attend a band festival on the other side of the state. Mr. Peiffer drove us there. We left very early in the morning and drove for what seemed like an eternity. On our arrival, we had dinner at a restaurant near the host school. After dinner we decided to take a walk around the town to stretch our legs after that interminably long car ride. We walked and talked for a good couple of hours. The conversation was filled with dreams, hopes, aspirations and worries. Mr. Peiffer spoke of how wonderful life, teaching and music were and how bright and successful he was sure our lives would be. He gave me confidence and counsel. As long as I may live, I will never forget that walk or that conversation. I have replayed it time and time again. That was Mr. Peiffer. What a gem of a person. I always respected and cherished him, even when I was mad at him, and I hope he sensed how much I appreciated him. I hope I thanked him enough. But I know in my heart, I never really did.

After graduating from high school and moving on to college, I spent many moments thinking of Mr. Peiffer, with most of that time spent realizing how much I owed to him and how I really needed to sit down and thank him. As that feeling grew, I planned a trip home with the intent of taking Mr. Peiffer out to lunch and finally getting that chance to truly express my appreciation for all he had given me. I was very excited. I drove home, pulled into the driveway of my parent's house, walked up to the front door where I was met with a big kiss and hug from my mom. But I could tell something was wrong. She handed me a note, and told me that she had received a phone call to let us know that Mr. Peiffer had died suddenly. I was devastated. I was so very saddened at the thought of his passing, but I was more upset at the thought that he had died without my ever getting the chance to say "thank you." That opportunity was now gone forever. Even all these years later, I realize Mr. Peiffer—always the teacher—though no longer with us, had taught me a valuable lesson: Never put off thanking someone when you have the chance, for that chance may disappear forever.

I tell that story to every honors band I conduct. I ask all of them to go home and thank *their* music teachers. I tell them that whether it is with a note or a pat on the back, they need to thank the people who helped make them *who* and *what* they are today. I tell them *not* to make the same mistake I made. Sadly, though, many young people are shy or have trouble expressing themselves in words. So as I come to a close, I would like to take this opportunity to express to you what each and every one of your students wants to say, but like me, probably never took the time to say:

Thank you for being you.
Thank you for being there when I needed someone to talk with about a problem.
Thank you for making me strive to be a better person as well as a better musician.
Thank you for showing me how to be dedicated.
Thank you for allowing me to sense wonder, emotion, awe and joy.
Thank you for caring.

Thank you for always giving of yourself.

Thank you for helping me learn to cry.

Thank you for allowing me to grow.

Thank you for showing me what it meant to be a teacher.

Thank you for being dedicated.

Thank you for being honorable.

Thank you for being enthusiastic.

Thank you for all the extra time you gave me.

Thank you for showing me the joys of music and of life.

Thank you for helping me at every juncture.

Thank you for your wisdom, poise, dignity and intensity.

Thank you for challenging me.

Thank you for never giving up on me even when I gave you reason to.

Thank you for never letting me be less than what I could be.

Thank you for seeing the vision of my successes in the future, rather than my failures of the past.

Thank you for helping me to become what I am and will be.

Thank you for giving me a sense of pride and worth.

Thank you for showing me the beauty of truth.

Thank you for being you, my teacher.

Goodbye, Mr. Peiffer. I miss you. I hope you know what you meant to me. But I know the best way to honor you is to become the best teacher I can be. I only hope someday to mean as much to one person as you did to me.

POSTLUDE

Pablo Picasso once affirmed, "Everything you can imagine is real." Who more than a teacher can understand the truth of that simple statement or the responsibility in its message? For we have dedicated ourselves to *imagining* what our students can become and to helping them make it real. Day by day, challenge by challenge, step by step, we help each of them accomplish what started in the imagination as a hope, a wish, a dream.

Let us never lose sight of that goal. Let us never stop seeing what isn't there, seeing what our students can become. Let us never forget those amazing, remarkable words of Henry David Thoreau: "The question is not what you look at, but what you see."

Each of us chose music—or maybe music chose us. We are music teachers; it is what we do and who we are. It is our passion. It is our purpose. Our life's work begins with little dots placed on five lines and four spaces. It ends with lives that are changed forever. What we teach is as much about what is felt as what is heard, as much about what *cannot* be expressed in words as what is said. We help young people to see what is invisible, and to know what can't be understood. We help them to develop their skills as much as their hearts and souls. We are music teachers; it's just what we do. For those who have dedicated their lives to this calling, no explanation is necessary. For those who have not, no explanation can suffice. Maybe Blaise Pascal said it best: "The heart has its reasons which reason knows not of."

And now, I can think of no better way to end this book than with the words of Albert Pike who stated, "What we do for ourselves dies with us. What we do for others remains, and is immortal." Each of you shares your talents, skills, knowledge, love and compassion with your students. Each of you shares yourself, your heart and soul. And that gift will live on for generation after generation to come and touch the lives of those you will never know.

May the passion you have for music and teaching ever strengthen your purpose. May your dedication to your students be matched only by the joy they bring you. May you spend all the days of your life cherishing the wonder that is you, and the profound impact you have on all those you teach. Walk with them, excite them, empower them, make them curious, push them, and gently invite them to grow. For that is your passion, it is your calling, it is your mission, it is your *purpose*.

"Without you, there never would have been..."

About the Author

Peter Loel Boonshaft, also author of *Teaching Music with Passion*, holds Bachelor of Music (Summa Cum Laude), Master of Music Education in Conducting and Doctor of Musical Arts degrees. Dr. Boonshaft also was awarded a Connecticut General Fellowship for study at the Kodály Musical Training Institute, from which he holds a Certificate. He is currently on the faculty of Hofstra University in Hempstead, New York, where he is Professor of Music, Director of Bands and Director of the graduate wind conducting program. He was Founder and Music Director of the Pennsylvania Youth Honors Concert Band and the Connecticut Valley Youth Wind Ensemble, and held the post of Music Director and Conductor of the Metropolitan Wind Symphony of Boston.

Dr. Boonshaft was selected three times as a National Endowment for the Arts "Artist in Residence." He has received official proclamations from the Governors of four states, a Certificate of Appreciation from former President Ronald Reagan, and has performed for former President George Bush, former President

Bill Clinton, and former Prime Minister Margaret Thatcher. Extremely active as a guest conductor and speaker for conferences and festivals nationally and internationally, he was chosen as guest conductor of the MENC All-Eastern Band, MENC All-Northwest Band, Goldman Memorial Band, and was named conductor of the MENC National High School Honors Band. He has been keynote speaker for the National Convention of the American String Teachers Association, the European Music Educators Association, the National Convention of the American School Band Directors Association, the MENC Southern Division, and the MENC Northwest Division. ▊